M000265967

Southern Comfort

Copyright © 2004 Shellie Rushing Tomlinson

All Rights Reserved

ISBN 0-9712259-5-8

Published 2004

Published by All Things Southern 2007 Island Point Drive Lake Providence, LA 71254.All rights reserved. No part of this publication may be reproduced, stored in a retrieval system, or transmitted in any form or by any means, electronic, mechanical, recording or otherwise, without the prior written permission of the author.

Manufactured in the United States of America

Southern Comfort

Shellie Rushing Tomlinson

Dedicated to the porchers
of the *All Things Southern* Community.
http://www.allthingssouthern.com

Table of Contents

Southern Comfort

Introduction

Several years ago, I was an interior decorator a basketball coach, *and* a "closet" writer. I credit my kids with pulling me out of that closet. My sisters and I used to tell our kids stories about our childhood—just like every other family—but strangely enough, my teenagers didn't get tired of hearing 'em. They even began to ask me to write 'em down, so they could remember them for their kids. And that is when my first book was born, *"Lessons Learned on Bull Run Road."*

Seeing the need to market my writing, I decided to launch a website. My entire marketing plan could be summed up into two ideas; I'd send out a FREE weekly emag to attract visitors, then I'd sell my books and other products in the online store. I considered opening a site that would reflect my faith in God, but I wanted everyone to be comfortable in my corner of cyber space. I figured if I opened a "Christian" site, the only people that would pause there would be Christians. Because my next great passion is the south and the Delta in particular—the birth of *All Things Southern* was almost automatic.

All Things Southern has five weekly features, beginning with my porch chat—which is just me rambling. After that, I add a southern joke, quotes, recipe and "my southern comfort." I chat with the world about everything else, and when we're all comfortable, I slip in a little inspiration. The folks that subscribe to my FREE weekly emag are called "porchers" and we porchers are having fun. You can join us by subscribing at www.allthingssouthern.com.

Since the birth of *All Things Southern*, I've been on a quite a journey. *ATS* is now a toddler, and like every toddler I've ever known, she's into everything! In addition to my cyber porch, *ATS* has grown into a radio and television show with me as your happy hostess.

Over the last few years, I've had many readers and listeners ask me to compile my Friday features, *"The Southern Comfort"*, into a book. You're holding the result of that kind request in your hands. Regardless of whether you are a follower of Christ or just a curious onlooker, I hope you find The Source of All Comfort between these covers. And I hope you'll come see me afterwards if you need to chat. I'll be on the porch…

Hugs,
Shellie

"Coming Clean"

One terribly hot summer day, when my sisters and I were little girls, we decided to build ourselves a swimming pool behind my daddy's tractor shed. We must've dug most of the afternoon before Cyndie, my oldest sister and consequently the foreman, deemed the hole to be large enough. The three of us pulled the water hose over to the hole and turned on the faucet.

I still remember our disappointment with the mud hole that developed instead of the crystal blue pool we'd envisioned. I know what you're thinking—silly little girls…What we needed was a clean container, not a dirty trench. But, don't we adults do the same thing? No? Are you sure?

How many of us try to clean up on our own, thinking that God can't use us until we're as clear and pretty as chlorinated water? So we try, in vain, to give up our bad habits and obsessions with this world's dirt.

Consider the alcoholic trying to resist another drink. There he is shoveling temptation over his head as fast as he can, while bucketfuls of desire slide down around his feet. And how about the lady trying to exchange her cigarette habit for a carrot stick? She's a closet smoker; her own kids don't even know she smokes. Or do they? If she can just quit, it'll be her secret forever. Maybe so, but she'll grow rabbit ears before that wedge of veggie gives her the hit

1

she craves. Of course, you're not like them. You're addiction free. But, what about that bitterness you feel toward your parents? You can't go to church until you've forgiven them, right? Wrong!

God doesn't expect us to come to Him all clean and shiny. He knows better than we that such an expectation is impossible. He just wants us to come—asking for forgiveness. He's the only one that can clean our containers and fill them up with Living Water. It's never too late for God to take what we are and make us what we were meant to be.

Shellie Rushing Tomlinson

*It's never too late for
God to take what we are
and make us what we
were meant to be.*

3

"The Alpha and the Omega"

For some time now, my habit has been to spend a few minutes in each of my kids' rooms each morning, praying for them. One Monday morning not too long ago, I was sitting on Phillip's bed praying about the knee surgery he was scheduled to have that coming Wednesday. About the time I said the word "Wednesday", I heard these words in my heart, "I'm already in Wednesday." I don't know if the thought was mine, or a whisper from the heavens, but it brought instant comfort.

I know, it's not exactly a news flash. You already knew He is the Alpha and Omega, the Beginning and the End. You know He isn't constrained by time. But, do you take this awareness and wring out all the good you can from it?

When I was a little girl, riding the bus home from Transylvania Elementary School, I looked forward to seeing Mama's face at the carport door. It didn't matter if I had a belly-ache and a ton of homework; it always felt better knowing Mama was already there, waiting on me.

The next time you find yourself dreading something in the future, I encourage you to dwell on the truth that God is already there. It feels good, try it.

Shellie Rushing Tomlinson

*I hope you're not
dreading the future;
God's already there.*

5

"The Art of Communication"

When Phillip and Jessica were born neither of them could talk. Can you believe that? It irritated me. It was even worse when they began to form silly little syllables like "ma-ma" and "da-da". I'm telling you, I had no patience for it. I decided right then not to give them a single thing they asked for until they could learn to ask for it correctly! Jessica, being the oldest, eventually learned to talk before Phillip and that was nice. After that, I didn't care if he learned or not. I mean, I could always just talk to Jessica.

Ridiculous, you say! Was I crazy? No, I'm just trying to make a point. I didn't really respond that way at all. On the contrary, like you, I hung on every sound my babies made. Why, when they began to talk in one and two word sentences, I couldn't have been more impressed by the world's best orators.

I think you see where I'm going with this, don't you? We can act so silly sometimes. A lot of people say they don't pray because they don't know how or what they should say. They act as if their Father is going to respond like that make-believe me above.

The Word teaches otherwise. It says our prayers are a delight to the Father—just like the first words of our kids are to us. Our children learned to talk one word at a time. If they had never spoken because it was too hard to master the language, they'd be handicapped now without the ability to communicate. Instead, because they did learn to express themselves, we've been able to communicate. My husband, Phil, and I have had some delightful conversations with them, (and some that weren't so delightful, if you know what I mean.) Nevertheless, we've been able to answer their questions, explain to them about the world around them, and guide them as they grew up.

If you're a baby Christian, or maybe a believer who's never developed a prayer life, there's no time like the present. I urge you to begin now to talk to your Father. Yeah, He has a lot of kids to talk to and I'm sure Billy Graham and the Pope can both talk His ear off. But you know what? They can't take your place and He's waiting to talk just to you.

There is no one else who
can take your place.
Your Heavenly Father
is waiting, just for you!

~*~

"Letting Go of the Dock"

I remember when we were little girls and my family would go water skiing at a friend's house on Lake St. John. My older sister, Rhonda, was deathly afraid of the water. I can still see her wearing a big orange ski-vest, with a life-belt around her waist for good measure, straddling a raft and clinging to the dock. All the while Mama would be patiently trying to get her to come out to the floating deck where the rest of us were laughing and playing.

Steadfastly opposed to the idea, Rhonda would be crying and pouting, holding onto the ladder with a vise-grip. I don't know what bothered Rhonda more, the unseen things beneath the murky water or the extremely remote chance of actually drowning. The reality was she was so buoyant it would've taken a real-life sea monster to pull her under.

I'm not bringing this up just to pick on my sister, (although picking on my sisters is always fun). No, I thought about Rhonda's irrational fear the other day because I've been able to relate recently. I wish there were time to get into the details, but for the sake of today's chat, let's just say the Lord has been calling me in a new direction and it's been one forevermore scary move.

Don't grin at me. I'm not the only camper the Lord is "calling out into the deep" these days. The Lord asks us to walk by faith and not by sight. He wants all of us to let go of the things we "think"

9

are keeping our lives afloat and trust in Him for protection and provision.

Let's see...I've got the Word, His Promises and His Spirit. Now if I could just let go of the dock…

Shellie Rushing Tomlinson

Let go of the Dock!
Release the things you
think are keeping you afloat
and trust in Him for
protection and provision.

11

"Who Are You, Really?"

When I was little, I couldn't talk right. If you could hear my country voice, you might think I still can't. But, I'm not talking accents here, I mean, I could not talk clearly. I've always loved to tell stories, but the only person in my family that could understand me was my older sister, Cyndie, and she wasn't the most reliable translator—sorry, Cyndie.

This problem was hard at home, but then I went to school and my embarrassment quadrupled. When I was in the second grade, a speech therapist used to come to the door of our class once a week and call for the speech kids—and all the kids in my class would turn around and chant in a sing-song voice, "Speech kids, speech kids." It's safe to say this therapist wasn't on my Christmas list.

I never dreamed I could make a living writing stories, let alone telling them out loud, but that's the direction the Lord has decided to take me in. He has a plan for your life, too, and your strengths and weaknesses are all part of the package. Don't be afraid and don't allow the world to say who you are. Why not go straight to the Source? Ask the One that created you who you are and what you were meant to be!

Shellie Rushing Tomlinson

*If you're wondering
who you really are,
don't listen to the world.
Go straight to the Source.
Ask your Creator!*

"Recess—God's Way"

Ding! Ding! Recess! Remember how good that bell sounded in grade school? Just for a second, try to recapture the anticipation you felt when you heard it. Got it? Good! That's the feeling God wants to give you right smack in the middle of whatever circumstance you find yourself in. God knows you need a break and he is inviting you to enter into His rest.

As wonderful as recess was, it didn't call off the spelling test or magically complete your math problems. What it did was refresh you and reenergize you for those tasks. God's rest works the same way. It won't blow the reality of your situation away like the seeds of a dandelion, but it will equip you to face them.

The writer of Hebrews says, "He who has entered into God's rest has ceased from the weariness and pain of their human labors." That's taken from my amplified Bible. I'm pretty familiar with that weariness thing, aren't you?

Entering into God's rest is available to us all through faith, the leaning of your entire human personality on Him in absolute trust and confidence in his power, wisdom, and goodness. Unfortunately, sometimes we get too busy to hear the bell! Just think of it as recess—God's way.

Shellie Rushing Tomlinson

*Entering into God's rest
is available to us all.
It's recess—God's way!*

"A Winning Tip"

As an athlete, I love a good, fair game. But there is one rigged playing field I want to warn you about.

Let's say a new job opportunity has opened up for you. You've been praying for something in this field and now you feel like the Lord is leading you to take it. Enter the opposition—that enemy of your soul, Old Slew Foot. "What if," he says, "your kids don't like the new school?" Your comeback is strong, but he doesn't relent. "What if you don't like it, after all and you can't go back?" This time, your answer is slightly weaker. Now, he circles in for the kill. "What if you move your whole family and then lose the job?" Ah, ha! He's got 'cha! Now you're second-guessing yourself and you can't remember if God's in this thing or not.

Can I tell you how to win the game of "What If"? Don't play it! Just don't play. Slew foot has had 2000 years of practice playing this game. He's better at it than you are. It doesn't matter how many "what ifs" you answer—he'll always have another. If God has given you direction, listen to Him and Him alone. Stay focused in what God is doing today. Tomorrow isn't guaranteed anyway.

Shellie Rushing Tomlinson

Stay focused in what
God is doing today.
Tomorrow isn't
guaranteed anyway.

"Thank You Notes"

Here in the South, we send thank you notes for birthday, Christmas, graduation, wedding and baby gifts, just to name a few. Every southern bride is aware that the speed and content of her "thank yous" reflect directly on the family she comes from and the one she's marrying into. We also write notes for expressions of condolences or hospitality.

Unfortunately, as well brought up as we are, we often fail to say thank you to the One who gives us our greatest gift—life and it's many blessings. Many years ago ten lepers were healed and only one turned back to give thanks. His "thank you note" got the Lord's attention. He even put it in the Bible.

The Word tells us to give thanks, and not just before our evening meal. Maybe, like me, you've been guilty of neglecting a "thank you". A whispered prayer was answered. You're grateful, and you're enjoying the gift, but you just never got around to expressing your appreciation. If so, why not stop right now and dash off a note, thanking the Lord for His provision. Like our mamas would say, "Even a belated thank you is better than none at all."

Shellie Rushing Tomlinson

*Are you caught up
with your thank you notes?
Remember, even a belated thank you
is better than none at all.*

"Would that be Weakness or Obedience?"

I had an interesting talk with a close friend yesterday. He was talking about his workplace and how difficult the week had been. My friend has a great sense of humor and comedic timing so, of course, he made the story funny. "You know," he said. "I try to be kind, to help others, to not respond in anger, and all those things, but my co-workers don't see it as Jesus. They see it as weakness. All they see is a sucker."

I know where he's coming from. Don't you? We all have people that push our buttons. Southerners would say "This is where the rubber hits the road." These are the folks that force us to choose whether we're going to do things our way, or His way. Sure, it'd be easier and a lot more fun if we could say, "You know, Sally, the only reason I'm not slapping you upside the head is because I love Jesus." Unfortunately, we won't win many people to Jesus that way.

I'm thinking about the time the disciples asked Jesus how many times they had to forgive someone that wronged them. His response was seventy times seven. Mercy! That could look like a whole lot of weakness, couldn't it? Maybe, but maybe Jesus was reminding us of something he knew that we'd like to forget. What finally gets people's attention isn't your talk, but your walk. Not a single incident of kindness, but a lifetime of putting others first.

Can we wrap this up with a promise? Last week at Vacation Bible School we taught the kids that people look on the outside, but the Lord looks on the inside. I'm trying to remember the same lesson. In other words, Sally isn't the one keeping score. The sixth chapter of Matthew has tons to say about this, but for brevity's sake, let's just look at verse thirty-five: "Love your enemies, do good ... hoping for nothing in return, and your reward will be great..." And here's the promise. What the world might see as weakness, the Lord sees as obedience—obedience He promises to reward.

*It's never your talk—
it's always your walk,
that eventually
gets their attention.*

"Kingdom Principle"

I want to tell you about a kingdom principle I've found. Suppose someone you love has hurt you and you want an apology. No, you need an apology. Different versions of this battle have been raging for some time and you're fed up! Still, because you desperately want a better relationship with this person, you've made it a matter or prayer. Good! But what else are you doing?

Are you "withholding" yourself from them emotionally until you get that well deserved apology, determined not to let them off the hook before they learn their lesson? I understand. The last thing you want to do is condone their actions and you're afraid that if you forgive and forget they might never change, right? You're just trying to help.

But, does God need this kind of help? Or do our actions reveal our lack of trust in His response? I believe we tap into an awesome spiritual principle when we forgive without first requiring an apology. It seems when we combine our prayers with faith and return to being the sibling, friend or spouse we're called to be, we remove ourselves from the equation and break the pattern of conflict. Think about it this way. When our loved one isn't engaged in verbal battle with us, how much easier will it be for them to hear the real Teacher?

We tap into an awesome spiritual power when we forgive without first requiring an apology.

"Are we there yet?"

I remember one inevitable question from all the trips of my childhood. "Are we there yet?"

My Papa loved seeing the different parts of our country and he wanted my sisters and me to appreciate it, too. All we could think about was the destination. Papa wanted us to relax and enjoy the scenery. He was planning on getting us there, but he wanted us to see and learn some things along the way. Mama encouraged us to bring books and toys to occupy our time. Instead, my sisters and I occupied ourselves by dividing the backseat into thirds and threatening anyone who crossed the line with even the toe of their flip flop.

Reminds me of some Christians I've known. They talk a lot about having their ticket to heaven, but they sure don't seem to be enjoying the trip. Do you see 'em? That's them riding in God's back seat with a somber look on their face, making life as difficult as possible for people going the opposite direction as well as those traveling right with 'em.

The Bible says, "This is the Day the Lord has made, let us rejoice and be glad in it." That's not just for Sundays! Lighten up folks, we're called to reconcile the world and take others with us. That's going to be hard to do if we look like we're marching to Zion...with a rock in our shoe.

*Some Christians talk a lot
about having their ticket to
heaven, but they sure don't seem
to be enjoying the trip!*

"My Refuge"

There are many kinds of places to go to for help these days. There are all types of half-way houses, overnight shelters, and support groups; and let me be quick to say that the majority of them are doing a fantastic job. But, may I recommend mine? It's advertised in the Bible in the 48th chapter of Psalms. It's called "Mount Zion and its situated on the sides of the north. It's the city of a great King." You can find that in Psalms 48. The psalmist goes on to say that God has made himself known in the palace for a refugee.

Myself, I go to Mount Zion daily. Many times I'm bruised and wounded from the realities of life. But I like it best when I'm not there for therapy. On those days I like to skip around the palace and explore the rooms. There are so many that have never been opened; I find something new every day. So, if you're looking for some lasting help, I urge you to go to Mount Zion. Oh yeah, and if you don't know the way—give me a holler—I've got directions.

*There are many places to
go to for assistance,
but if you're looking for
lasting help—you're looking
for Mount Zion, the city
of the great King.*

"No Place to Dump"

Several years ago there was a ship in the news that appeared to be on an endless voyage. One after another, the ports it contacted refused it permission to dock. As far as I know, it could still be out there. The ship was full of trash that no one wanted.

Excuse me if this sounds personal, but where do you dump your trash? Not the garbage bags in your utility room, I'm talking about the emotional refuse we all accumulate—that jagged memory of rejection, that sticky feeling of failure, that dirty wad of guilt. Even if the situations that produced the feelings have been prayed over and forgiven, their images can still spring to mind and surprise you with their ability to torture.

Unless you're paying by the hour, few people are interested in this baggage. Although some kind-hearted folks will allow you to "rest" your load on them temporarily, even the best of friends can grow weary of continual dumping.

Enough, already—here's the good news! I know from experience, that Jesus is always willing to listen. I give him those painful thoughts every time they float into my consciousness and every single time He gives me peace in exchange. What a deal! Try it friends, the only thing you stand to lose is a load of trash no one wants in the first place!

Give those painful thoughts to Jesus. The only think you stand to lose is trash no one wants in the first place...

"Taking Names"

I don't know if they still do this today. When I was in elementary school and the teacher had to leave the room, she always appointed someone to take the names of anyone who talked while she was out. I was never chosen; I can't imagine why. I can still see the appointee standing at the board, chalk in hand and arm poised with a double dog dare attitude on their face. It was a "make my day" type of thing that Clint Eastwood would've been proud of. Of course, the boys in the class had to cough or clear their throat to prove that they could cross the noise barrier without repercussion.

I want to read you a scripture in Malachi that made me think about the whole "taking names" thing. It's found in Chapter Three, verse sixteen. "Then those who feared the Lord talked often one to another; and the Lord listened and heard it, and a book of remembrance was written before Him of those who reverenced and worshipfully feared the Lord and thought on His name."

How cool is that? When you and I talk about the Lord, He's listening and taking names. And the best part? He writes in ink. Now, that's a list I want to be on. How about you?

Southern Comfort

When you and I
talk about the Lord, He
listens and takes names.
How cool is that?

"A Picture of Grace"

I have a picture in my head of a news story that hit the wires several years ago. Although I don't remember all the details, I remember that it focused on the rescue of a young autistic boy, maybe seven or eight years old, who climbed to the top of a very tall electrical tower, oblivious to the danger all around him. Although my heart ached for the little boy, the part of the story that really touched me was the reaction of his older brother.

The child's brother, a teenager at the time, was afraid of heights. Imagine the fear that must have gripped him when he saw his little brother perched precariously on that steel beam. And yet, the older boy was so scared his little brother was going to fall, he climbed to the top of the intimidating tower and held onto his sibling until the rescue workers arrived. I remember the autistic boy sitting there, without ever acknowledging his brother's presence, while the older brother held him firmly and protected him from a sure fate. There is a beautiful picture of grace in that story. Can you see it?

Jesus struggled with his mission in the garden of Gethsemane. He asked his Father to take the cup from Him several times. The inevitable suffering of the crucifixion was not as painful to him as the separation from God that would come as a result of taking on the sins of the world. And yet, in the end, knowing that his death on the cross would mean life for us, Jesus accepted his assignment with the words, "Not my will, but thine, Lord."

Just like the older brother in our story, Jesus came to save us—and just like the younger boy, we didn't even know we needed saving when our rescuer began to climb the cross. The older boy rescued his brother out of unconditional love, not a prior relationship, for the younger was incapable of such give and take of emotion that usually precedes loyalty. I John 4:19 says, "We love Him because He first loved us."

The little boy needed a savior—his older brother was there. Two thousand years ago, Jesus knew that one day, you and I would need a Savior. Have you told Him that you're thankful He was there?

Shellie Rushing Tomlinson

He came to save us
before we knew
we needed saving.

"Intimate Belief"

Although I was seldom separated from my kids when they were babies, the times I did have to leave them, our reunions smacked of desperation. They'd cling to my neck and inhale my scent as if their very next breath came from me. I knew there was no one that could take my place. My sister's little girl took it even further. Up until she was about a year old, Hillary Joyce would throw up if she couldn't have her mommy.

Did you know that we've got a Father in heaven yearning for that type of relationship with us? While it's certainly true that in exchange for our belief, we're offered an abundant life now and eternal life later, my amplified Bible paints a more complete picture of just what it means to believe. Listen to the familiar words of John 3:16. "For God so loved the world that he even gave up His only begotten, unique, Son, so that whoever believes in, (trusts in, clings to and relies on), Him shall not perish but have everlasting life."

Do you see it? Let's get a picture of ourselves clinging to the Father's neck. It's not just what He wants, it's what *we* need.

Shellie Rushing Tomlinson

Trust in, cling to,
and rely on—
a complete picture
of what it means to believe.

"Rules or Relationship"

"Step on a crack, break your mama's back." That was just one of the rules that governed our childhood play. There's no way my mama can appreciate the lengths my sisters and I went to in order to protect her vertebrae. It was a hard rule to follow. Once you start looking, there are cracks everywhere!

Of course, that was childhood. We adults don't have rules like that, right? Wrong! I've known Christians who are all about rules. The problem is this, rules equal religion and religion doesn't satisfy the hungry soul of man, a relationship with the Father does. Let me give you some good news and a promise.

The good news comes from Micah 6:8. "He has showed you, O man, what is good; and what does the Lord require of you but to do justly, to love mercy, and to walk humbly with the Lord your God."

And here's the promise. If you actively pursue an intimate relationship with the Lord, He'll let you know what He likes and dislikes and—I'm quoting now—"His yoke is easy and His burden is light!" You know...I'm bigger now! I might just go find a crack and step on it!

Shellie Rushing Tomlinson

*Rules equal religion
and religion doesn't satisfy
the hungry soul of man...*

"Not So Secret Hideout"

I remember extended family Thanksgiving meals at Grandmaw Stone's in Natchez, Mississippi. While the women slaved in the kitchen, Cousin Lisa, my sister Rhonda and I would wait beneath the tablecloth in the dining room for the arrival of the big bird. Our turkey wasn't served Norman Rockwell style. He was sliced and brought to the dining room with the other dishes.

As the culinary efforts of the women mounted, the smell above our heads became unbearable. We held our breath and watched the legs of the cooks come and go, taking turns darting out for a sliver of the bird and diving back beneath the table for cover. Turkey has never been so good! Inevitably, or so we thought, we'd soon slip up and leave a foot or hand showing—payday!

Years later I was told our hideout wasn't as secret as we'd thought. We were just ignored until our parents decided the game had gone on long enough.

An innocent childhood game for sure, but it reminds me of a serious adult one. Have you ever thought you were getting away with something, hiding it really well from everyone who knows you? Guess what? Hebrews 4:13 teaches us that nothing we do is concealed from God, but that everything is open and exposed to His eyes. Hmmm...I don't know if you're hiding something or not. That's between you and the Father. Just remember—if you are, your foot's showing...

Shellie Rushing Tomlinson

Nothing is hidden
from God;
everything is
exposed to His eyes...

41

"The Trouble with Tomorrow"

There is a priceless work of art framed and hanging on the wall of my hall bathroom. Jessica drew it for her brother, Phillip, when she was about five and a half. Phillip was four at the time and had busted his mouth open playing (not a rare thing for him, unfortunately). I doubt my guests have ever recognized the raw talent this mother saw all those years ago in her little girl's artwork, but no one has ever read the crooked crayon lettering without smiling. "Dear Phillip," she writes. "I hope you feel better tomorrow. I love you. I will help you pick up your toys tomorrow." And then once more, to make sure he's clear on the time frame, she reiterates, "I will help you tomorrow. Get better soon. Jessica."

It's easy to laugh at Jessica's well-meaning procrastination. It's a little harder to recognize the same pattern in our own lives. "Tomorrow I'm going to read my Bible more. Tomorrow I'm going to volunteer more. Tomorrow I'm going to pray more." We can all fill in the blank with our own good intentions. The trouble is none of us are promised tomorrow. We only have today.

Shellie Rushing Tomlinson

~*~

*What are you promising
to do tomorrow that
you should be doing today?*

~*~

"Right Standing with God"

So, you want to be in right standing with God? Good, Jesus said our righteousness had to exceed the righteousness of the scribes and Pharisees. Uh, Oh! Hit the brakes! Have you ever looked at what the Pharisees did? They followed the law to the letter! And we're supposed to top that? Yes, we are, but it's easier than you think.

Read Matthew Chapters 9-12. In these verses we find some very angry Pharisees. They're horrified because Jesus' disciples are eating and drinking with people the Pharisees consider to be sinners. A few verses later, they're even more amazed to see the disciples eating the Temple Bread—and on a Sunday, at that! Why, they would have never done such things. There were many, many laws and regulations in the law. The Pharisees had studied them all and Jesus' guys were breaking a couple of big ones. And then, as if that wasn't enough, Jesus really stirred them up by saying his disciples were guiltless—that the Pharisees were the guilty ones. What was going on here?

It's simple. The Pharisees had religion; they considered themselves righteous because of their careful law-keeping. In contrast, the disciples had a relationship. They recognized that Jesus was Lord—over the rules, the temple, and the Sabbath. Their obedience, born of love, started in the heart. They had learned that sacrifice without obedience was worthless—and because they were committed to obedience, Jesus said they were guiltless. Wow!

Can you see it? Our righteousness (or right-standing with God) can top that of the Pharisees. It can—if we're interested more in a love relationship with Christ that the empty observance of rituals. If we try to keep Christ's commandments without a relationship with Him, we'll find them as burdensome as the Pharisees did. On the other hand, if we seek to know Him and let Him write His laws in our hearts we'll want to keep His commandments because we love the Commander. Jesus called this right-standing. I call it the best news I've heard in a while.

Sacrifice without
obedience is worthless.
Obedience sacrifice
is priceless.

"Making Lists"

Oh, hi porchers, I was just sitting here on the swing making my Christmas lists. I've got several going. There's my shopping list, cooking list, things to do list—why, a few minutes ago I caught myself making a list of the lists I need to make.

Okay, I'm joking about that last one, but I do want to tell y'all about one list I've learned not to work on. This morning I was reading out of my new Amplified Bible. I've always loved the 48th chapter of Psalms. It speaks of exploring Mount Zion, the city of the Great King, and it says that God has made Himself known in her palaces as a Refuge. Nice, huh? But here's the thing that caught my attention. In verse 13, right after we're told to share our faith with the following generation, there's a phrase instructing us to "cease recalling disappointments."

Uh, oh, I'm afraid I've been guilty of recalling disappointments. Heck, I've even listed our family's recent woes for anyone willing to sit still long enough to listen. But not anymore—I'm a reformed list maker. Now, who wants to join me for a rousing chorus of "Count your Many Blessings"?

*What type of list
are you making?*

"Beneath His Wings"

Even though both of my children are in college, when they're hurt or sad I have flashbacks to their "little kid" faces. I want to comfort them and chase their troubles away. Fortunately for me, we have a good relationship and they generally let me help, (or at least they let me think I'm helping anyway). I can't imagine how I'd feel if they shut me out.

Allow me to show you a scripture in Matthew 23:37. Jesus is speaking and His words really grab me. "Oh Jerusalem, Oh Jerusalem...how often I would have gathered you as a hen gathers her chickens under her wings—but you were not willing." Please indulge me here and reread that scripture with your name in the place of Jerusalem. Did you do it? Wow! How about that? God wants to hold you close and kiss your skinned knees and bruised elbows. I hope you're not shutting Him out.

*God longs to hold
you close and kiss
your skinned knees.
Are you willing?*

"God's Inside Voice"

How I wish I could just hear a big booming voice when I need an answer from God. You know—the hand on the wall type of thing. I've been thinking...our occasional lack of communication, mine and God's; do you think it's on His end or mine? Yeah, that's what I decided, too. God chooses not to compete with all the other noise in my life. In His wisdom He knows that getting louder isn't the answer. I had a teacher in elementary school that always lowered her voice when we were rowdy. The louder we were, the softer she talked. But, she knew something! Invariably, we'd pipe down to hear what she was saying. I've decided God uses His inside voice for this same reason—so I'll get still and listen.

So, I've been practicing listening to God. Most of us make a lot of decisions every single day. The majority of them are small, not your life-changing, this-better-be-a-good-one type of decision. That's fine; I'm using these little ones to sharpen my listening skills. When I need to decide between this and that, (example: how many t-shirts to order), I ask God to tell me which answer would be best. Guess what? I still don't get the booming voice, but most of the time the answer I come to feels right, like it's already settled and I just found out. The way I see it—the more I listen, the better I'll be at hearing when I have a more serious question.

Maybe this sounds like nonsense to you. Maybe God speaks to you in His outside voice. If not, if your hearing tends to be dull sometimes, too—I urge you to practice on the little things. It works! Go ahead, "bother" Him; He loves it.

Shellie Rushing Tomlinson

*I've decided that God
uses His inside voice
so I'll get still and listen...*

~*~

"God's Version of DSL"

Mind if I vent? I have a friend that calls me almost every morning. I like her, but the girl has no listening skills. As soon as I pick up the phone she starts talking and when she gets through—why, that's it. She hangs up before I can say much of anything. Oh, and if we don't get to talk in the morning, she won't speak to me the rest of the day. I can try to call her, but she doesn't answer. If I want to talk, I have to wait until the next morning's "chat", if you can call it that.

I bet you think my friend's rude, huh? Well, guess what? I made her up. She doesn't exist, not exactly. I wanted you to meet her because that's the way I used to pray. Every morning I'd have what I liked to call my "quiet time" with the Lord. Only, it wasn't so quiet. I rambled the entire time like my imaginary friend. When I got through, I hung up the phone and got on with my day. But, then I learned that the Lord wanted more than a scheduled "quiet time" with me. He wanted a quiet and peaceable life for me, born out of continual fellowship with Him. It's an attitude of having your face turned towards the Father throughout the day, leaving the line open at all times. Think of it as God's version of DSL...always on. It's where you'll find the intimacy with God that our human spirits hunger for. Try it, you'll like it.

Shellie Rushing Tomlinson

~*~

*The Lord wants more than
a quiet time "with" you.
He wants a quiet life "for" you.*

~*~

"Who's in Charge?"

Not long ago I saw a cartoon of a very small boy being pulled down the sidewalk by a huge Great Dane. The little boy was trying his best to pull back on the leash, all the while shouting, "Now, let's get this straight. You are my dog! I am not your boy!"

As cute as this picture is, I see a sobering resemblance here to someone I know really well. Myself! Sometimes when I say all the right things, do all the right things and pray all the right prayers and still don't get my way—I can get a little like this young man. Of course, I'd never say it out loud, but my ugly attitude dares to whisper to God, "I'm not your servant. You're my God!"

So, maybe I'm preaching to myself here and you've never dared get so uppity with our Father. Well, someone else did. Why else would the Bible have said in Romans 9:20, "Nay, but O Man, who art thou that talks back to God?"

God isn't a formula. He's the Creator. We can't control God with our repetitious prayers any more than our young fella above can control his dog with a lease. We're talking about the Father of all time here, the First and the Last, the Maker of heaven and earth. I think our best response when we don't get what we want can be summed up in two words, "Yes, sir."

Shellie Rushing Tomlinson

~*~

God isn't a formula;
He is the One who formed us...

~*~

"A Babe, a Man and a King"

It's Christmas Eve, the sweetest day of the year. Before another Christmas comes and goes, and you start packing up the decorations and sweeping the needles off the rug, I want to tell you a little story.

Long, long, ago, a baby was born in Bethlehem, a long awaited King, wise men came to worship and angels came to sing. The babe became a child one day and lived in Galilee; he grew in favor with God and man in the land beside the sea. A man came to Jerusalem to set his people free—the crowds rebelled in anger we have no place for thee. A babe they kissed in Bethlehem, a boy they watched with pride, but a carpenter's son in Jerusalem—this man they crucified. A babe was fine in Bethlehem and a child in Galilee, but a Messiah for Jerusalem? They found no place for thee.

I hope this story challenges all of us not to put away the Christ Child with our lights and ornaments. That baby grew into a man and that man shed His blood for us at Calvary. There's a brand new year ahead of us, let's all share it with the Messiah.

*A babe was fine in Bethlehem
and a child in Galilee,
but a Messiah for Jerusalem?
They found no place for thee.*

"The Secret to Successful Resolutions"

As a child growing up on Bull Run Road, New Year's Eve meant out-of-town company! Each year my parents' friends would make the two-hour trip from Natchez, Mississippi to celebrate. Although our festivities were pretty tame, we could get rowdy—especially during the spoon game when the utensils dwindled and the players tensed.

At midnight, Papa would shoot his rifle in the air and we kids would holler while the adults kissed and the big, silver ball dropped in New York City on our black and white TV in the corner. New York was light years away from Bull Run Road, but the big city celebrants and our gravel road group all had one thing in common—the promise of the New Year.

I know we've all shared in this scenario many times since, and I bet we can agree that each year more resolutions and goals are set than are ever kept. And that's why I want to give you a head start this year, a secret that will help you meet your goals. It's found in Proverbs 16:3 and it reads, "Roll your thoughts upon the Lord, (commit and trust them to Him; He will cause your thoughts to become agreeable to His will), and so shall your plans be established and succeed."

Shellie Rushing Tomlinson

Roll your thoughts
upon the Lord,
(commit and trust them
to Him; He will cause your
thoughts to become
agreeable to His will),
and so shall your plans
be established and succeed."

Proverbs 16:3

"Cleaning House"

I'm thinking of something I enjoy more than decorating the house for Christmas. Can y'all guess what it is? If you said "taking down the Christmas decorations", you're a winner! Last Friday the feeling hit me as soon as I opened my eyes. By that afternoon, anything and everything even remotely tied to the holidays had been boxed up. I had vacuumed, dusted and cleaned like a crazy woman and the whole house was back in order. I hate to brag, but it was spotless. And it stayed that way for oh, I don't know, at least thirty minutes before the men came back from hunting, Jessica got in a cooking mood in the kitchen and Rocky stamped his dirty paws over the carpet headed for his spot in front of the fireplace.

My house reminds me of something else I have trouble keeping clean. Maybe you can identify. I'm a grateful Christian, thankful for the salvation God provides through His son, Jesus. I enjoy going to church, reading my Bible, and praying. I have good intentions. Unfortunately, just when I think I'm all cleaned up, my old nature resurfaces and I trip up again. But that's enough bad news—I want to leave you with the Good News! It's found in First John Chapter One. "If we say that we have no sin, we deceive ourselves and the truth's not in us. If we confess our sins, He's faithful and just to forgive us our sins, and cleanse us from all unrighteousness." Has your heart gotten dirty? Let the Lord clean you up. It feels good!

Shellie Rushing Tomlinson

Keeping your heart clean
is not unlike keeping
your home clean.
You have to be committed to
the daily housework.

63

"Who's Your Daddy?"

Can I ask you a personal question? You don't have to answer out loud. Okay, here goes. Do you ever envy people that seem to know God personally, in a way you're not familiar with? You want to know the Lord, but you don't feel that connection. I'd like to help, if you'd let me.

You've probably heard me talk about my kids, Jessica and Phillip. I'm blessed to have a great relationship with both of them. But let's just suppose this wasn't the case. I'll even give you a hypothetical good reason for our hypothetical problem. Let's say that from their birth they had stayed with everyone but me. They played at Aunt Rhonda's in the morning, visited Aunt Cyndie in the evening and slept at Nanee's at night. They wouldn't have been very familiar with my voice or my ways, would they? Do you think they'd be a little confused as to whom they really belonged to? I do.

A relationship with the Father is like that. Salvation is a free gift from God. If you've ever recognized you needed Jesus and asked Him into your heart, you were born into the family of God. However, if you don't spend time with Him, you'll never be confident about that—ever! And you'll miss out on the abundant life He has for you. On the other hand, if you do spend time with Him, you'll be able to say with the Psalmist, "My Father is God and I will exalt Him."

Shellie Rushing Tomlinson

Who's your Daddy?

"Keeping Promises"

I remember when Mama would reach her boiling point with my sisters and me. "I promise you one thing," she'd say. "If I hear one more argument today, nobody's going to be able to sit down for a week." As I grew up I began to realize that not everyone took a promise as seriously as Mama did.

There are plenty of folks that will give you their word and not think twice about going back on it. Kinda makes it hard to trust people, doesn't it? Of course, if we're honest with ourselves, we'll have to admit that we've all broken a promise or two in the past. So, who can be trusted? Oh, I thought you'd never ask.

Did you know that 2700 times in the Old Testament God the Father is identified by the Hebrew name, Jehovah Elohim? It's a name that means covenant-keeping God, the God that can be trusted to keep His promises. The 23rd verse of Lamentations chapter three reads, "Your mercies are new every morning. Great and abundant is your stability and faithfulness."

The bottom line is to have faith in God. You can trust Him to keep His promise.

Shellie Rushing Tomlinson

Jehovah Elohim, a
covenant-keeping God
who can be trusted
to keep His promises.

"Turning the Tables"

When I was a little girl growing up in the South I heard a lot about blue runner snakes. The old people said that if you're being chased by a blue runner snake you can stop and turn on it and it will run from you. To a little country girl like myself this sounded fantastic—just like that you could go from being the chased to the chaser. There was a part of me that always wanted to test this story, but just a small part. Unfortunately for me, (or fortunately, whichever it might be), I never got chased by a blue runner.

Thinking about those blue runners reminded me of the enemy of our souls—that old serpent the Devil, the great pretender. He just loves to bombard us with fears and worries and threats, or maybe reminders of something we've long since received forgiveness for.

But just like the blue runner snake, there's a way to send the Devil packing when he comes chasing at your heels. The Bible says in I Peter 5:8, "Satan, AS a roaring lion...seeks whom he may devour". I put the word "AS" in capital letters because a wise preacher once showed me this scripture and told me to remember that the Devil couldn't devour me like a roaring lion, he could only pretend to. The Bible also says in Revelations that we overcome the enemy by the word of the Lamb and the power of our testimony.

Now, we're getting somewhere! The secret is to use God's word on him. Try it the next time that old snake comes slithering your way.

Shellie Rushing Tomlinson

Quote him a little Bible, or sing him a little scriptural song. I can't say for sure about blue-runners but, on the authority of God's word, I can confidently say Satan is one snake that will flee!

Southern Comfort

*Your enemy isn't
a roaring lion,
he just sounds like one.*

"Mercy, Not Sacrifice"

I was studying in Matthew, Chapter Nine, when I read these words: "Go and learn what this means, I will have mercy and not sacrifice." I admit, I kept reading with barely a pause.

A few verses later Jesus repeated himself, but this time with an admonition for not following his earlier advice. "IF, (emphasis mine), you had known what this meant: 'I will have mercy and not sacrifice, you wouldn't have condemned the guiltless.'" Suddenly, it didn't sound like a bad idea to spend some time "going and learning." My understanding is far from complete, but I'll tell you what I've found so far.

At first I thought of "mercy" as just being willing to overlook wrongs. But, in studying the original Greek, I discovered that "mercy"as it's used here, goes a little further, suggesting a loyal act of love or devotion born out of a prior relationship, especially a covenant relationship. Mercy isn't just an internal feeling and sacrifice isn't just an external action; there's a relationship between the two. Maybe an analogy will help to explain it.

If you're a parent, chances are you've found yourself, at least once, watching a great performance known as the "The Noble Martyr", starring your own little darling. (Maybe you've even starred in this role a few times yourself.) It's a role requiring the actor or actress to go to great lengths to portray the sacrifices of obedience. I know

Southern Comfort

I've seen my little stars perform a household chore, like folding
clothes, complete with heavy sighs and drooping shoulders that
were meant to cause me—their audience—to appreciate their great
sacrifice of time and energy. Unfortunately for them, their
dramatics never inspired a great rush of gratitude, but rather a
certain amount of irritation.

Now, if we can replay the same scene a little differently...This time
you come in from work and the same child is folding the same
clothes—but now she's doing it because she knows you're tired and
there is still supper to cook and chores to do. You recognize that
she is doing this out of her relationship and love for you, her
parent. At this point you leave immediately to go buy her a car.
(Just joking!)

There's a lot more to this one. For now, let's wrap it up this way.
When our relationship with Jesus is so intimate that we obey His
commands out of love and not duty, we'll meet the approval of the
only audience that really matters—an audience of One.

Shellie Rushing Tomlinson

Obedience is born
out of intimacy.

~*~

"Listen To Learn"

A lot of people don't read the Bible because they say it's too hard to understand. I can relate. Let me tell you a story. I've got a new friend that came to my house a couple days ago as a complete stranger. This fellow is a freelance computer consultant, (you can read that as "bonafide genius"). You should see what he did with my limping Dell—it's skipping around like a brand new puppy.

Which brings me to back to my point...As much as I instantly liked Blaine; we had a tiny communication problem. He speaks fluent geek—I don't. When Blaine talked about my computer's insides I must have looked a lot like our dog, Rocky, does when we're teaching him something new. Blaine would read my expression and smile. Then he would back up to square one and break it down for me in simpler terms. The more I listened, the more I understood.

Bible study works that way. Listen to this promise from Hebrews. "I'll put my laws into their mind and write them in their hearts and I will be their God and they will be my people. It won't be necessary for one to teach his neighbor to know me, for all will know Me, from the smallest to the greatest."

You can do it folks. Get into His word and give the Lord a chance to speak to you. The more you listen, the more you'll understand.

Shellie Rushing Tomlinson

*Give the Bible a chance.
The more you listen,
the more you understand.*

"Don't Say I Didn't Warn You"

This is not an emergency. If it were an actual emergency, I wouldn't be here. Okay, I'm just kidding. This is only a warning, a warning to any porchers out there that feel overworked and underpaid and are considering having a pity party. Do not—and I repeat do not read from the book of Hebrews, and especially not from an Amplified Bible. Your party will be a washout.

Hebrew tells us to be satisfied with our present circumstances and with what we have for God Himself has said, "I will not, I will not, I will not in any degree leave you helpless nor forsake you nor let you down, nor relax my hold on, assuredly not."

See what I mean, porchers? I was practically working on the menu for my pity party when I accidentally read this passage today. So, whatever you do, be careful with Hebrews, or you just might find yourself saying crazy things like, "Thank you Lord" and smiling at people that haven't done anything but bug you.

Shellie Rushing Tomlinson

~*~

*Nothing can bust up
a good pity party
like a bit of Bible reading...*

~*~

"Fighting Back—God's Way"

I was sitting at a red light beside a schoolyard last week, when I noticed a big boy pushing and taunting a smaller child. All the while the little boy was holding a big stick in his hand. Each time the little guy got up, the bigger boy pushed him down again. Just as I started to get involved, the bell rang rescuing the little boy—at least temporarily. I drove away worrying about the child and secretly wishing he would've just whacked the big boy. I know he wanted the problem to go away. But I also knew that until he stood up for himself, the bully wasn't going to stop. It made me think about the rest of us and the spiritual battle we're born into, whether we like it or not.

Let me explain. Are you out of sorts, worried, depressed? Guess where all those bad thoughts come from! I Peter teaches us that we have an adversary, the devil. Matthew says he comes to steal, kill and destroy. This bully loves to load us down with the cares of this world. But, here's the good news. Hebrews says, "The word of God is quick and living and sharper than any two-edged sword." That's a big stick over there on your nightstand, porchers. What are you waiting for? Find you a good verse and hit him with it.

*We can't choose whether or
not to participate in this life's
spiritual battle; we're born into it.
We can choose to overcome the
enemy of our soul with the weapon
God has so faithfully provided.*

"Owning Up"

I wasn't much bigger than a tadpole when I figured out that Papa
and Mama valued honesty a lot more than my sisters and I did. I
remember Mama staring me down. "Isn't there something you want
to tell me," she'd ask. That always struck fear in my heart. What
did she know and, better yet, how much should I tell her?
Memories of my recent infractions would flood my mind. Of
course, there was always the outside chance that she was fishing
for information. Sometimes I took a chance and tried to play
innocent. This never worked out well. Not owning up to my
misdeeds often cost me more than the original offense.

I can't help but liken this memory to the Bible passage that
describes Jesus as the tried and precious cornerstone of our faith.
And yet the 21st chapter of Matthew clearly warns, "Whoever falls
on this stone shall be broken to pieces, but he on whom It falls will
be crushed to powder."

Can I give you a heads-up porchers? When you hear God's still
small voice saying, "Isn't there something you want to tell me", go
ahead and 'fess up. Just like my experiences with Mama, you'd be
better off falling on His mercy now than facing His judgment later.

Shellie Rushing Tomlinson

*Not owning up to your deeds
can often cost you more
than the original offense...*

"Living Apart, Dying Alone"

About a month ago, I pulled down a lot of English Ivy from some trees along my driveway. (I thought it was pretty, but my husband was worried that it was choking the trees. Don't you think that's a myth?) Anyway, it was a pretty big job. Even though I was able to pull a good bit down in large pieces, some of the vines broke off up high out of my reach. Instead of getting a ladder, I chose to take the lazy way out and leave it there, figuring it would die soon enough.

Do you know that for the longest it looked like that ivy was just fine? It was just as pretty as the other ivy that was still attached to the ground. It was pretty and green and still trailing beautifully around the tree trunks. I noticed it from time to time and decided it must be getting enough nutrients from the tree itself, and that being cut off from the ground wasn't going to hurt it after all.

Boy was I wrong! Although their death was gradual, even imperceptible at first, the vines are now dry and brown, graveyard dead. This, of course, got me to thinking.

Jesus said that He is the vine and we are the branches and that our life is in Him. Put another way, we're just like the ivy. We can quit relying on the Source for a little while and everything looks fine. We can skip church, miss our Bible reading, neglect our prayer time and all the while the world will think we're just as spiritually healthy as the guy beside us.

The hard truth is, just like the ivy got its nourishment from its roots, our spirits are fed by God. If we try to live without His sustenance, the day will come when our spirits will dry up and die. Will we know in time? Do we really want to take the chance? I say, let's dig our roots in now, while we have the opportunity. I want to keep growing, don't you?

*Living without His
sustenance is
really dying without
His sustenance.
It's just not as obvious
to the naked eye.*

"Handling Our Emotions"

My son's basketball team is headed to the state tourney. It's been a wild ride! Our team doesn't win any games comfortably—they're all basket for basket, last second wins. Whatever happens from here, our boys' greatest strength has been their ability to handle these roller-coaster games. Had they celebrated with every point they scored or moped after every bucket from the opposition, (like we parents do), they wouldn't have gotten this far.

Sounds like real life, huh? There's always another disappointment ahead and there's always another encouraging moment. Christians aren't immune to this roller coaster. And yet, our great privilege is being able to take these emotions to our Heavenly Father. Our challenge is to submit our emotions to Him so that we can accept the good and the bad without losing our focus or becoming too depressed to help the team.

The Apostle Paul understood this and said, "I've learned in whatsoever state I'm in to be content." I've had opportunities to learn this lesson myself here at *All Things Southern* lately. I may not be the smartest kid in the class, but thankfully, I have a very patient Teacher.

*There's always another
disappointment ahead and
there's always another
encouraging moment.
Our great privilege is being
able to take these emotions to
our Heavenly Father.*

"Hard Work—It's a Good Thing"

We chopped a lot of cotton back on Bull Run Road, and hoed a ton of beans. Sometimes, when the sun was high in the sky and my shirt was drenched in sweat, and the end of the row was nowhere to be found—the sight of another stalk of Johnson Grass was overwhelming. You couldn't skip it; Papa always saw the weeds you missed. Still, if we worked hard, Papa was faithful with our paychecks, a dollar an hour—big money at the time. Papa always said hard work never hurt anyone.

Did you know the Bible also speaks highly of the hard worker— and frowns on the lazy? Our weariness comes when we work and struggle without regard to the Eternal One who gave us Life. Ecclesiastes says, "Whatsoever your hand finds to do, do it with all your might." Papa kept a cooler of ice water waiting for us girls at the end of the row and it felt good all the way down! But consider this, Corinthians says, "Eye hasn't seen, ear heard, or heart imagined what our Heavenly Father has for those who love Him? Come on folks; let's worship while we work—the Boss will love it!

*Eye hasn't seen or ear
heard what the Father has
planned for those who love Him.
Wow, what a payday!*

~*~

"God Sees in the Dark"

Even though my kids are grown, I can easily recall their childhood fears. I remember them calling out to their Dad and me when a storm would hit and knock the electricity out, sending their rooms into pitch darkness. They tried to sound calm, but you could always tell they were on the verge of panicking. "We're here," we'd call to them. "Just stay where you are and we'll come to you." Our voices soothed them instantly.

Most of us are too grown up now to be scared of the weather. And yet, none of us are above panicking during a personal crisis. Maybe you're hearing the crashing thunder of financial woes or health problems, or maybe the flashes of war on our horizon frighten you. I'd like to encourage you to stop and holler for your Heavenly Father. But before I do, let me give you something to think about. My children were comforted by our response because they recognized our voices when we called out to them. In the same way, we need to pursue a relationship with our Heavenly Father and learn to recognize His voice so that when the storm hits and the lights go out, we can call out to Him in confidence. And the best part—God sees in the dark.

*Are there scary shadows and
frightening noises in your life?
Don't forget! God sees in the dark...*

~*~

"Are You Ever Homesick?"

The hallway in my home is filled with family portraits. When my guests pause to look at them, I beam with pride! It reminds me of another hallway found in the eleventh chapter of Hebrews.

It's called the Hall of Faith. I like to think of it as God's Photo Gallery, filled with portraits of some of His kids. There's David and Moses and Gideon—just to name a few. These guys whipped lions, parted the Red Sea and defied entire armies. And yet, there's a neat sentence tucked in the 16th verse that gives the criteria for inclusion in God's gallery and these mighty feats aren't mentioned. Instead, it explains that these people knew there was another world past this one, and they yearned for that heavenly home they would one day share with the Father. For that reason the Bible says, and I'm quoting now, "God is not ashamed to be called their God, as in the God of Abraham, Isaac and Jacob, for he has prepared a city for them." Can't you just see God beaming as He scans His photo gallery? Clearly, the Lord wants us to live, love, and serve others while we're here on this earth, but it's also obvious that it warms His big old heart when we get a little homesick.

Smile...
you're in
God's photo album.

~*~

"The God Spot"

Have you heard? In the last few years there's been a lot of talk about scientists finding the "God Spot." Some experts believe they've isolated the place in our brain where we communicate with God.

Tests were run by injecting radioactive dye into the brains of people while they were praying, tracing it and photographing the results with a high tech imaging camera. They found that when people pray they have significantly increased activity in the frontal lobe of the brain and decreased activity in the rest of the brain. They concluded that the right temporal lobe of the human brain is wired to receive signals from what some are calling a "Grand Organizing Design" or G.O.D.

With all due respect to these great scientists, they aren't the first to come upon this revelation. Centuries ago, the preacher of Ecclesiastes was moved to say in Chapter 3:11 that "God has set eternity in the hearts of men."

I believe he was saying that God has set in each of us an awareness that we're all eternal beings, that deep down everyone knows there's more to life that the brief flash we see as people live and die in a seemingly endless parade of humanity. I believe that along with this recognition comes a desire for the "rest of the story" or a "God Spot" if you will.

Of course, not all of the scientists agree with the "God Spot" theory. Some dismiss it outright. I'm fine with that. I like the way Professor Haught expresses it: "Faith is the sense of being grasped by this higher dimension...or deeper reality...If we could come up with clear proof or an absolutely mathematically lucid verification of deity...that wouldn't be deity—it'd be something smaller than us." (Well said, Professor Haught!)

So, I guess my question is: What have you been trying to fit into your God Spot? I'm reminded of the story of Goldilocks and the Three Bears. Have you tried to cram material things into the void in your heart? Too tight! Have you tried to fill it with family and friends? Better, but something is still missing. What about a relationship with the Father? Ah....just right. Wow! God in the God Spot—what a comfortable fit.

Shellie Rushing Tomlinson

What are you trying to fit into your God Spot?

"Unrealistic Expectations"

In my efforts to lose a few pounds before bathing suit season, I've recently tried the low-carb diet—waging an all out battle against sugar and fat calories. I'm pretty sure it'd work if I didn't spend so much time rubbing shoulders with the enemy.

The other day I ordered a Grilled Chicken sandwich, determined to eat the meat and discard the bun. "You want fries with that?" the voice asked. "Why not," I answered, "and supersize 'em while you're at it." Just kidding! I wasn't that weak! It'd be pretty unrealistic of me to think this will work if I eat all the bread, pasta and sugar I want one minute and go low carb the next.

You know what else is unrealistic? Sometimes we expect our Sunday church attendance to transform our lives. Now, don't get huffy. I'm not pointing fingers. We're all in this together. All I'm saying is, if we truly want our relationship with the Lord to make a difference in our lives, we need to spend some time with Him every day, and not just one out of seven.

Shellie Rushing Tomlinson

Expecting one-day-a week
church attendance to
transform our lives
without a daily relationship
with the Father, is like expecting
a morning grapefruit to offset
six days of fast food.

~*~

"Sitting in Daddy's Lap"

When Jessica and Phillip were toddlers, I learned to allow a certain amount of lap time after waking them before I could expect them to bathe or face breakfast. They'd curl up in the recliner with me in their footed pajamas and watch morning cartoons through sleepy, sand-filled eyes. Rushing either of them before sufficient lap time started everyone's day off in an ill humor.

I've developed a similar habit lately that is having that same type of positive effect on my mornings. When the alarm rings, or Phil announces that it's time to get up, I lay there a moment and curl up in my heavenly Father's lap. For a few minutes, without opening my eyes, I just rest on His shoulder. This is most definitely not my prayer time. I'm usually too sleepy or overwhelmed with the thoughts of all I need to do that day. It's just a way of turning my face towards Him and starting my day off with the recognition that He is my comfort, my inspiration and my reason for being. It's a good feeling and somehow the day doesn't seem quite as overwhelming—regardless of what's on the list.

Shellie Rushing Tomlinson

Starting each day by
turning your face
to the Fathers
can turn dreaded tasks
into desirable activities...

"Reclaiming the Day of Rest"

When my children were toddlers, I was a strict enforcer of "naptime." Every day I saw to it that they slept for a short while after lunch. The little tricycle motors never embraced the idea. They knew what they wanted. "Me don't wanna nap," they would each protest, while rubbing their heavy eyes with chubby fists. But I knew what they needed. They'd be much better equipped to handle the afternoon or evening's activities after a little shuteye.

Our Heavenly Father knows us even better than we know our children. He created us, and He knows just what we can handle and how far our human legs can take us. That's why He built a special naptime into our weeks. It's even known as the "day of rest." You guessed it. I'm talking about Sunday, also known as the Sabbath. The trouble is few of us use it as a day of rest anymore. We know what we want—we want to catch up on the yard, the paperwork, the house chores, etc...But our Heavenly Father knows what we need: a day of worship and rest. I bet if we'd go back to doing it His way, we'd be much more equipped to handle the next week's activities, don't you think?

Shellie Rushing Tomlinson

*Our Heavenly Father
built a "grownup"
naptime into each week.
It's even called,
"The day of rest."*

101

"Liar, Liar, Pants on Fire"

I couldn't decide if I was watching the news or a late night comedy show. There was Iraq's information minister, denying that Coalition forces had taken the Sadaam Insane International Airport while insisting that the Iraqis were going to take it back. Uh— pardon me, Saeed. Which one is it? I'm reminded of what the late Jerry Clower once said about one of the Ledbetters, "Anybody that knows Newgene knows the boy is a registered, bonafide, world class liar." Move over, Newgene. This Saeed guy would rather climb a tree and tell a lie than stand on the ground and tell the truth.

The Bible has a lot to say about lying but the verse I find most interesting is found in Proverbs 12:17. It reads, "He who breathes out truth shows forth righteousness." There's an interesting choice of verbs. Instead of just speaking the truth, this person breathes the truth. Breathing is involuntary; you don't have to think about it. Wouldn't that be great, if we all just breathed the truth? I believe it can happen—when we pursue a relationship with Jesus, who is the Truth. The problem lies, (no pun intended), in our willingness to bend the facts. If we fudge the story a little today, eventually we won't mind totally fabricating it tomorrow. You know what's scary about that, don't you? We could end up like Old Saeed, a fellow who wouldn't recognize the truth if it jumped up and bit him on the behind!

~*~

*If we fudge the story
a little today,
eventually we won't mind
fabricating it a lot
tomorrow...*

~*~

"Grading on the Curve"

I remember my first response back in high school when our test papers were returned and I saw a disheartening grade on mine. I'd look around quickly.

"Hey Ronald Lee," I'd whisper. "What'd you get?" Then I'd turn to Leslee, "What'd you make?" As bad as it sounds I was hoping for the worse. Mind you, I never asked Edward "Never Made a "B" in his Life" Yee. It wasn't just the misery loves company thing. If enough of us had done poorly we'd try to convince Mrs. Sullivan to grade on the curve. This could turn a "D" into a "C' and a "C" into and "B", unless of course she based the scale on Edward. If that happened we were all sunk!

Sometimes it seems it'd help if God graded on the curve. I know a few folks I stack up pretty well against. But then again, if Mother Teresa is setting the scale, I'm in deep trouble. The truth is I'm glad God chose to set up one sure standard for all of us. At the end of our lives, we'll be judged on whether or not we, as individuals, accepted Jesus and followed his teachings. The thoughts and actions of our friends and neighbors won't even figure into it. It's more than fair—it's justice from the One true judge.

Shellie Rushing Tomlinson

~*~

*Unfortunately,
God doesn't grade
on the curve!*

~*~

"Temper Tantrums"

When my son was small he'd come home from school and launch into an account of the wrongs he'd suffered during the recess football game and how terribly angry he'd gotten at his friends. Phillip knew his temper was wrong. He was always asking me to pray with him for the Lord to take it away. I tried to teach him that although it was fine for us to ask for help, most of the time the Lord doesn't zap our shortcomings. He wants us to learn by obedience.

It was experience talking. So, where did you think Phillip got it? After years of struggling with my own temper, one day I read in Proverbs that if you rescue an angry man, you'll have to rescue him again and again. I realized that the Lord was saying that I needed to learn to recognize the things that set me off and control my own reactions. If God would've zapped my anger, I wouldn't have learned to re-program my response and He would've had to zap all my other faults as well. Proverbs also says he who has no rule over his own spirit is like a city that's broken down without walls. It's true. When we fly off in anger, we open ourselves up to other problems. Of course, Phillip and I still blow up at times, but we've both improved a lot since we accepted the truth that whatever angers you, controls you.

Shellie Rushing Tomlinson

~*~

Whatever angers you,
controls you...

107

"Wisdom Anyone?"

I don't know about you, so I'll just be speaking for myself here as a wife, mother, and business owner. I need wisdom. Every day of my life, situations arise and choices present themselves to me that require wise decisions. Thank goodness, I know where the well is.

James 1:5 says, "If any of you lack wisdom, let him ask of God, that giveth to all men liberally, and upbraideth not; and it shall be given him."

Can you believe there have been times when I've warned my kids about something—and they did it anyway? I know. And then they come to me, finally, truly repentant and asking for help. It's always tempting to dish out my advice with a healthy dose of "I told you so." Of course, they don't need to hear that dreaded line. They remember my warnings. They come to me hoping for a little direction without pouring salt in the wounds of their dilemma.

Instead of saying "I told you so", I try to remember how my Father treats me when I'm dealing with my kids. Let's read the verse from James again. But this time, let's read it concentrating on the word "upbraid". Webster says the word means, "To criticize severely, to scold vehemently." Did you reread it? Wow! It gets sweeter and sweeter, doesn't it? Help without condemnation; what a concept!

I think the wisdom the Lord gives is not always how to avoid the tests and trials of this life. Sometimes it's wisdom to learn how to

Shellie Rushing Tomlinson

learn from the experience as well as directions on extricating yourself. Yes, I know what you're thinking. If I followed His instructions, (from the Bible), I might not find myself in as many pickles. You're right...

He upbraids not...I ask. I ask all the time.

Help without condemnation?
I ask...I ask all the time!

~*~

"Drinking from the Well of Inspiration"

I was out in my back yard early this morning, trying to rescue some suffering Crepe Myrtles. I had transplanted 'em right before I left town for a few days and they looked bad, like they'd drawn their last breath of carbon dioxide. I watered them really well though I didn't hold out much hope for their recovery. Well, guess what? A few minutes ago I took a peak out my kitchen window and got a pleasant surprise. Those Crepe Myrtles are perking up a little. While they're not ready for a House and Garden photo spread, I think they're going to make it.

I was reminded of how dry I can become if I let myself get too busy for my daily Bible readings. And just like me watering those unresponsive Crepe Myrtles, once I do sit down to read again, it feels sort of useless at first—like I'm just going through the motions. The good news is that I've found that if I will just commit myself to linger there, God will inevitably use His word to replenish my soul. Are you dry and thirsty? Find some time for a cool, long sip of inspiration from God's Holy Word. It comes highly recommended.

Lingering in the word will replenish your soul...

"All Together Now"

I was working at my computer enjoying the birds and squirrels feeding outside my window, when suddenly I heard an awful commotion. Glancing up, I noticed the birds squawking and hovering in mid air. That's when I saw the snake coiled around the feeder. He was trespassing and they were letting him know it. As the snake slid down, I moved slowly towards the bay window with my digital camera and raised it to get a clear shot. I expected the noise to scare him away. Instead he pulled his head up a good six inches off the ground and stared right back, almost like he was challenging me.

I believe those birds can help illustrate an important principle. As the moral fabric of our society unravels, the "anything goes" crowd demands that everyone "live and let live". And for the most part, we do. Maybe we're convinced that one lone voice for decency won't matter; maybe we don't want to be called extremists. But I'm reminded of the saying, "In a society where anything goes, everything eventually will." My mama always said you could disagree without being disagreeable and we're going to have to find a way to do just that. Remember—it was the combined warning of the offended birds that alerted me to the snake's presence. Our voices will echo and effect change, too, if and when we raise them together.

*Live and let live is
unraveling the fabric
of our society.
We can disagree
without being disagreeable.*

"On a Wish and a Prayer"

The diplomas were handed out, the cheers went up, the lights went down and the video began. Set to music, the pictures rolled by quickly, an irony that wasn't lost on us, their parents. Their first eighteen years had passed the same way. There they were in preschool, then first, second, and third. The faces slimmed down, the braces came off and they morphed before our eyes—the first homecoming dance, the big game, junior-senior prom. As I watched Phillip and his classmates begin their final processional, I realized that although the faces were different the emotions playing there were familiar.

You've seen them, the graduates that march with eager, assured steps and those that seem to amble with held breath, relieved to have someone ahead of them to follow. It's the difference between those that are prepared for what lies ahead, and those who are just hoping things will work out. We see the ones that are walking into the future on a wish and we shake our heads. We know that although life is good, it's hard, and harder still for those who aren't prepared. The challenge is to see ourselves in this picture.

One day, we'll all graduate into eternity. Some of will be prepared. We'll have made arrangements, built on a relationship with the Great Teacher. And some of us...some of us will walk into eternity on a wish.

*Don't walk into eternity
on a wish, but a prayer!*

"God is Just"

We've seen football stars move to the play-by-play booth, tennis greats doing color commentary and ex-White House officials hired as news correspondents. Obviously, experience is invaluable in the job market. So I guess maybe we should have expected this, but really—two TV networks have offered O.J. Simpson $40,000 to act as a commentator during the trial of accused wife-killer Robert Blake. Dare I say it? OJ stands to make a killing.

Okay, the truth is that regardless of what we think, none of us really know if OJ got away with murder. It's just that, at first glance, stories like this seem to contradict the lesson Papa taught on Bull Run Road. Papa said crime didn't pay and you know what? I still think he was right, because the Bible hasn't changed. It continues to read "whatsoever a man soweth, that shall he also reap."

My point is, don't let this type of thing discourage you from making the right choices. We'd all do well to remember that the Lord is keeping his own account and it's independent of our earthly judicial system. So, when you're confronted with a supposed injustice consider reminding yourself of something I've always told my kids, "Life isn't fair, but God is just."

*Life isn't fair
but
God is just!*

~*~

"The Deep Waters of Life"

That little trip I took with Papa last week sure made me nostalgic. I'm still thinking about long ago family vacations. I remember that our destination didn't matter a lot to my sisters and me—as long as we stayed in a hotel with a swimming pool. We'd run into our hotel room and change into our bathing suits lickety-split. Then we'd stand at the door and jump from foot to foot, bugging Papa and Mama to hurry into theirs. We laughed at Papa's farmer's tan, (dark brown arms and a lily white torso), but it didn't stop us from fighting to be the first in line to ride his shoulders in the swimming pool. Papa doesn't seem so very big now, but back then, he was a giant! I remember how secure I felt riding high above the water as he walked into the deep end.

My relationship with the Lord gives me that same feeling of security, and I want that for y'all. The book of Romans calls our Heavenly Father, "Abba", which is translated into "Daddy". You've got a strong, steady Father ready to support you in the deep waters of this life. Please don't go it alone.

*Security is walking
into the deep end
on your Father's shoulders!*

~*~

"Don't Even Think About It"

Wait right there! Don't do it. Don't even think about it!

Have you ever had an absolutely crazy idea pop in your head? Maybe you were just sitting there working when you thought about that cute guy in the next cubicle and how he looks at you...it's obvious he finds you attractive. You're flattered. Before you know it you're imagining another conversation with him, your little mental video camera supplying an accidental touch full of Hollywood tension, and then—whoa! In Scene Three you're kissing the dude in the break room! CUT! Where did that idea come from you wonder? You'd never do such a thing; you're happily married and you want to stay that way. Be careful.

How many times have you heard someone being interviewed say something like, "I never thought he'd do such a thing? He's not the type of person you'd think would hurt anyone." I'd be willing to bet the accused thought the same thing, once. But then he had a crazy idea, and he thought about it, and he considered it, and he dreamed about it—until one day it wasn't quite as abhorrent anymore.

Sadly, many people ruin their lives because they don't realize how our enemy works. The Devil's got his own twisted version of Johnny Appleseed going on, running around dropping bad thoughts into folks' heads.

Southern Comfort

It's harmless enough when the person receiving the thought realizes he wants no part of such a thing and immediately discards the notion. The problem comes if we dwell on it. For, the longer we consider it, the more possible it becomes. That's why the Bible says, "As you think in your heart, so are you." (That's Shellie's loose translation.) I don't believe this verse is talking about the occasional thought—but rather the pattern you allow to be established, the ideas you nurture.

Want a solution? Don't feed unwholesome thoughts, cut off their daydream supply and watch 'em die—before they grow up and choke you.

Shellie Rushing Tomlinson

The longer you consider
a bad idea
The more attractive
it becomes.

"Weathering the Crisis"

I like to say that my sisters and I were early versions of latchkey kids. When the weather was pretty, Mama locked the latch and we played outside. I remember my surprise when I tried to open the screen door and found it locked. Our next step—banging. Mama appeared mop in hand and smiled.

"Go play".
"But I'm hungry."
"Lunch is in an hour."
"But I'm thirsty."
"Use the water hose."
"But I'm tired."
"Go rest in the shade."

The woman was heartless. She could've opened the door but she wouldn't. Years later I had my own children and I began to understand that my kids would be healthier if they spent their free time playing outside rather than lying on the sofa in front of the TV. So, I learned to turn a deaf ear to a lot of their complaints.

So, do you think that could be why our Heavenly Father doesn't always intervene as soon as we start whining, I mean praying? Maybe He knows we'll be stronger once we weather the crisis. I'm not saying life has to be unbearable. Heavens no! Take a sip of refreshment from His holy water faucet and rest a spell in the shade of His favor. Before long, you'll be ready to join your siblings in the sun—and you'll be stronger for the experience.

Take a sip of refreshment
from His holy water faucet
and rest a spell
in the shade of His favor...

~*~

"The Living Word"

God's word is alive! It can breathe encouragement into conflict and victory into defeat. Try reading the Word like the lady searching for the lost coin. Expect the heavens to part and a thundering voice to speak to your need.

If I remember to read this way I always get more from my study time. One day I was searching the scriptures like this during a particularly trying time when a verse jumped out at me, and became so real to me, that I could almost believe the clouds had indeed parted. It was great! But the best part is that I can't quote this verse now without that feeling of peace returning to me.

Let me encourage you to read the Bible expectantly. Once a part of it becomes life to you—it will be yours forever. Care to know the verse that spoke to me that day? Micah 7:8: "When I fall, I shall arise and when I sit in darkness the Lord shall be a light unto me."

*Try reading the Word
like you would search
for something valuable—
it is!*

"I've Got People"

You've heard the expression. "I'll have my people call your people." I use it a lot as a joke. You see—I wear all the hats here at *All Things Southern* and it can get overwhelming. Sometimes I go from radio host to website operator to shipping manager in a matter of minutes.

Which is why I find John 14:16 so comforting that I've taped it up on my computer. Jesus is talking to his disciples and soothing their concerns about his upcoming death and resurrection and get this— He says I've got people! Okay, he doesn't exactly use those words. Let me read it to you, "And I will ask the Father and He will give you another Comforter." But that's not all; my amplified elaborates by saying that this Comforter would also be a Counselor, Helper, Intercessor, Advocate, Strengthener and Standby!

Maybe I don't have a staff of people. That's okay. I have a Divine Administration assisting me. And that same group is ready and willing to step into your lives. Cool, huh? Why don't you take a second and call the Board together? You'll enjoy the support, I know I do.

*Call the Board
together, folks!
You've got
People!*

"Telling on Papa"

I'm telling on Papa today. I can tell by your letters that y'all think life with my Papa was all fun and games. Well, things weren't always rosy on Bull Run Road. This past weekend set me to thinking about a particular Fourth of July when my sisters and I were in our early teens, harboring great hopes for the holiday. Cyndie had a friend whose family owned their own ski boat. Rhonda and I were hoping she'd be allowed to go to Billie Ruth's and we'd get to tag along. We were all excited about spending the day with our friends on the lake. Movie people would say we were "coming of age."

Papa didn't seem to care, for right about that time the corn and peas were coming of age themselves. Papa brought in bushels of produce and insisted it be put up that day—and this time none of our little girl pleading moved him. That year our Fourth was spent on the front porch with our lips ran out, fighting mosquitoes and shucking corn.

Now, y'all know I love Papa. I'm just bringing up the day he dashed our hopes so I can remind you of the hope that never disappoints. For brevity's sake, I'll jump into the middle of Romans Chapter 5. It reads, "And endurance develops maturity of character and confident hope of salvation. And such hope never disappoints us. For God's love has been poured out in our hearts." Isn't that beautiful? I urge you to reach out to The Hope that doesn't disappoint.

~*~

Reach out to
The Hope that
doesn't disappoint...

~*~

"If God is dead..."

I'm a news buff. If I haven't read the newspaper the day isn't done. Unfortunately, the news channels are far from what you'd describe as feel good entertainment.

More often than not, the news serves only to remind me of how much I treasure the reassurance my relationship with God brings. And then my thoughts progress to how difficult this world must be to those adrift without this stability in their lives.

How I wish everyone knew the wonder of having an intimate, personal relationship with God. Why? Does it make everything perfect? Heck, no! I could bend your ear with problems if I wanted to. Is it because it provides you with a heavenly reservation? Well, yeah, but that's the icing on the cake. The milk, eggs and flour are the peace, love and joy that come with the ticket.

My relationship with Jesus has given me a peace I couldn't find anywhere else. It's a settled feeling. Hebrews 6:19 calls it an anchor of the soul. I can't think of a better way to say it.

This past week I was looking for some particular song lyrics when I ran across an unfamiliar title. Although I've never heard the song, I could identify with the writer. The title was, "If God is Dead, Who's That Living in My Heart?" You know, on second thought, I think I'm going back to download those lyrics. I might've found a new theme song.

Shellie Rushing Tomlinson

*Salvation is a heavenly
reservation. Peace, love and joy
are the milk, eggs and flour
that comes with the ticket.*

"Knotted Shoelaces and Tangled Hair"

Even though my daughter Jessica is a mature twenty-year-old now, I often catch glimpses of the toddler she once was and I'm reminded of her personal mantra, "Me do it." I remember watching her struggle with things beyond her ability that I could've helped with. Instead "me do it" would get more and more frustrated. By the time she'd allow me to help, her shoelaces would be knotted beyond hope. And don't even ask how many hours I spent trying to untangle a comb from her hair!

With time, "Me do it" grew into "I know." It was even more painful watching her learn hard lessons I could've saved her from had she listened on the front end. It's a myth, you know, all lessons don't have to be learned the hard way! Some people figure out the stove is hot without burning their hand.

I don't know about you, but I can see myself in that picture of a willful toddler. I've found that one of the hardest lessons is learning how to walk daily with the Lord, listening for Him, and relying on Him before my shoelaces are knotted and the comb's tangled in m hair. It's easier to say, "Me do it" because we're taught that the world values independence. However, there's great benefit in understanding that the Lord values dependence. Once we realize that and submit to His lordship, life gets much easier. Why not try looking for Him before you make a mess out of things? Depend on

Shellie Rushing Tomlinson

His leading and see if things don't work out better for you. It does for me.

*There's great benefit
in understanding that the
Lord values dependence.*

"I Hear Voices"

During my evening walk the other day, I realized something. I hear voices—in my head—all the time. Now before you run for the white jacket you might want to hear me out.

You do, too! I see that expression. My mama would say, "Don't roll your eyes at me." We all hear voices. What's important is which voice we listen to and follow.

The Bible says the Lord has a still small one. It's a gentle voice that bids for your worship. Don't let that religious word intimidate you. Worship just means giving the Lord your allegiance and affection. The good news is when this Voice corrects it does so without crushing.

That's certainly not true of the other voice that's always in your ear. Satan is the original motor mouth. It's his voice that steers you down the wrong path and then makes you feel lower than a snake's belly for being there. The religious term here is condemnation and the Devil's fluent in it.

Our challenge is to learn to listen to the Voice that instructs and encourages us. God's voice will lead you to higher ground. Want to know more? Drop me a note. I'd love to help.

*It's Satan's voice that leads
you down the wrong path—
and then makes you feel
lower than a snake's belly
for being there.*

"Will Power or His Power"

"Go ahead, Shellie. Spill your milk so we can eat."

That's another of Papa's jokes from my accident-prone childhood.
He thought it was funny. Translated it meant, "We all know you're
going to spill your milk before we're through so why not get it over
with?" Mama would scold him for teasing me, and I'd determine
not to spill my milk. I remember picking up my glass very
carefully the first time, maybe even the second, and the third. But
inevitably I'd lose my focus and spill my milk before the biscuits
grew cold. So much for will power...

I think the Apostle Paul would understand. In the book of Romans,
he talks about doing the very things he doesn't want to do and not
doing the things he tries to will himself to do. Some people see this
as an excuse for giving in to the same old temptations. I don't think
that's what Paul meant at all. For right after that he asks—my
paraphrase here—"Who can deliver me from this vicious cycle?"
And then he answers his own question. Paul found the power to
live for Christ couldn't be found in his own will power or the latest
Christian self-help book but in a personal relationship with the
Lord. Living for Christ without living with Christ won't ever work.
If I may say so, you'll end up spilling your milk in spite of
yourself.

*Living for Christ
without
living with Christ
never works.*

"Diving in Headfirst"

I was stirring up some gravy for our evening meal, when my thoughts turned to my older sister's first gravy making experience. Mama was out of town helping a relative and twelve-year-old Cyndie was cooking supper. She did okay with the hamburger steak, but she wasn't clear on making gravy. Instead of draining most of the fat, Cyndie added a couple scoops of flour to the skillet of grease, filled it up with water and brought it all to a boil. That gravy had a top layer of grease similar to the greasy dishwater you see in those Dawn commercials—right before they find a leftover glass. Rhonda and I passed on gravy that evening but Papa took a healthy helping right onto his potatoes, casually asking Cyndie about her technique. Evidently, the gravy didn't have to be perfect; Papa was pleased with his daughter's heart.

That's a pretty picture of our Heavenly Father. He honors our intents as well as our actions. Is there something you've been wanting to do for Him? Perhaps you'd like to share your faith with your friends but you don't know how to start. Don't be nervous, follow Cyndie's lead and dive right in. You don't have to go to seminary to share God's love. So what if your gravy is a little greasy at first? It'll please your Father and you'll get better with practice. Oh, and Cyndie—she turned into a pretty good cook.

*You don't have to
go through Seminary
to share God's love.*

"Watch for Traps"

One day when my sisters and I were small we decided it was a good day for hunting. We weren't particular about the quarry—birds, rabbits, it was all the same. We didn't even want to kill our captives, just turn them into pets. With dogged determination we set out to build a trap like the ones we'd seen work famously in the Saturday Morning cartoons.

We took an old cardboard box and propped it up on one end with a sizable stick. Our bait came from Mama's kitchen when her back was turned. We attached one end of a long string to the stick and trailed the other to our hiding spot behind Daddy's pump shed. I can still remember us peeking out every second to see if we had any approaching suspects. To our great frustration, our family cat kept upturning our box and wrecking our hunt until she eventually wore down our resolve and caused up to give up.

If only the enemy of our soul was as obvious. Unfortunately, Old Slewfoot's been setting traps ever since Eve ran into one in the garden—and he's a lot smoother than my sisters and I were. His traps are better concealed.

Maybe you got in a fight with your spouse, and you just don't want to be the first to apologize, again. So, it's been days since you've spoken, no big deal, right? Or maybe you never argue at all, but you've allowed yourself to drift away emotionally. If you were able to see the end of that string you might be surprised. It could be a trap for your marriage...

Maybe you've been feeling sorry for yourself. Everyone else has it made! And you work so hard—why look at so-and-so, they don't even try to serve the Lord and look how great things are going for them. The Bible tells us that the joy of the Lord is our strength, hmmm...anyone after yours?

Although the naivety of our little girl trap might be charming, the scope of the Devil's plans is anything but. John 10:10 tells us the Devil comes to steal, kill and destroy. Come on folks; keep an eye out for those strings—especially the hidden ones.

"Surely in vain a net is spread in the sight of any bird." Proverbs 1:17

The Bible tells us
that the joy of the Lord
is our strength, hmmm—
is anyone after yours?

Getting Rid of the "Buts"

Here's a line that sticks in my memory from my teenage years with Mama. "Don't give me any buts". This was her reply when I tried to justify my willful rebellion. As in, "I know I shouldn't have, but all my friends were doing it." Yeah, this line of reasoning was always followed by the bridge-jumping debate at my house, too.

I think we Christians use the "but defense" a lot. We're guilty of saying things like, "I shouldn't say this, but..." Do you realize that when we use that phrase we're willfully choosing to do something we know we shouldn't? We're choosing our way over God's, our will over His and our Heavenly Father doesn't care for willful rebellion anymore than Mama did. Here's another sobering thought. There are eternal consequences for disobeying Him.

Are you ready for the Good News? Mama always forgave us— when we were truly repentant and not just sorry we'd been caught. And yet, her capacity to love and forgive doesn't begin to compare to that of our Heavenly Father's. The Bible teaches that if we'll confess our sins He'll be faithful and just to forgive us and cleanse us from all unrighteousness. And here's the best part: He'll choose to forget it ever happened. Mama's memory wasn't quite that short.

Shellie Rushing Tomlinson

~*~

*Choosing our will
over God's will
has eternal consequences...*

~*~

"Hope for Us All"

Back to school sales, book supplies, last minute vacations—everywhere I look are reminders that another school year is just around the corner. There they are in Wal-Mart, all the excited little faces carefully choosing just the right color lunchbox and notebook. Or maybe you've seen the older crowd; they try to look less enthusiastic—even downright grumpy if they can pull it off. But we know better. We've been there, haven't we?

Think back. Can you feel the excitement of that blank notebook, the promise that beckoned from the clean crisp paper? Last year's torn cover, smudged pages and less than perfect grades are just a memory. This year will be different. You're aiming high with a skip in your step.

Hold onto that feeling a minute. No, wait, hold onto it everyday of your life. Because that's the hope and promise your Heavenly Father wants you to feel in Him. Have you smudged a few pages of your life, torn a few covers, gotten more than a couple failing grades? I have. But there is promise available for us all! His blood can cleanse our souls; His word can renew our minds. Regardless of where you are, your Heavenly Father wants to hand you a brand new notebook. It's never too late to be the person God meant for you to be. And you can find that in His word: "I know the plans I have for you, for good and not for evil, to give you a future and a hope."

Shellie Rushing Tomlinson

*It's never too late
to be the person God
meant for you to be!*

"No Shining Splendor"

This week we'll observe the second anniversary of the 9-11 terrorist attack on the World Trade Center. As the horrific and heroic actions of that day are remembered, I know I will again think of how its legacy can be measured by how often we divide time by the phrases "before 9-11" and "after 9-11."

Our experience with the Father should have such a clear division, a time before we knew Him and after we started living for Him. So why is it that some people call themselves by the Father's name, but feel more like distant relatives? Let me show you a passage from the 50th chapter of Isaiah. I think it can help.

It reads, "Who is among you who reverently fears the Lord, who obeys the voice of His servant, yet who walks in darkness and deep trouble and has no shining splendor in his heart?"

Folks, that good man knows of the Lord. He's trying hard to serve, to adhere to all the rules he has ever heard, but instead of discovering the joy of the Lord, he's found only deep trouble. Don't despair, though, because the good news is found in the very next verse.

"Let him rely on, trust in, and be confident in the name of the Lord, and let him lean on and be supported by his God." Now, there's a picture of someone in relationship, who has searched God out, and found that He's even nearer than they first believed. So, obey the

152

rules, but spend time with the Ruler—that's the key to having shining splendor in your heart.

For shining splendor
in your heart—
spend time with
The Ruler...

"Monster Squash"

We had a rule when I was growing up. You didn't have to eat everything on your plate, but you did have to try a spoonful of whatever was offered. I remember holding a spoonful of squash in my hand and watching it as it morphed before my eyes, doubling and hanging over the sides of the spoon while mama pleaded with me to get it over with. Then it tripled until it obscured my vision. I looked around it and beside it to see if Cyndie and Rhonda were having any luck, only to meet their pitiful stares.

Back then I wondered why my parents put us through such torture. Now I know. They wanted us to have the nutrients from the veggies rather than the cavities from the candy we preferred. And they knew we'd never try the good stuff without a little outside pressure.

Sometimes our heavenly Father has to use a heavy hand to get our attention, too, but only because He has our best interest at heart. He wants us to know the strength and joy that comes through a relationship with Him and obedience to His word. Our stubborn resistance only deprives us of the eternal benefits of His nourishment.

Are you ready for the good news? Although I can't say Mama's squash got rave reviews after we forced it down, I can promise you, if you'll "taste" a relationship with your Father, you'll want another helping. And you'll be on the side of the Psalmist telling your own friends to, "Taste and see that the Lord is good."

Shellie Rushing Tomlinson

*Our stubborn resistance
only deprives us
of the eternal benefits
of His nourishment.*

157

"From the Creator to the Creation"

Growing up in the Delta afforded my sisters and me many opportunities to learn about the amazing animal kingdom. Here are a few facts. Skunks look like kitty cats when you're five but they aren't near as much fun. And when you get sprayed trying to pet the pretty cat it takes a lot of scrubbing before you can stay in the same room with everyone else. Chicken snakes don't bite, but they will scare the life out of you when you reach under the setting hens for the smooth, cool eggs, and grab their scaly bodies instead.

You can try to keep minnows until they turn into big fish but they'll always die first. Baby rats are cute but if you keep them in a coffee can and hide 'em in your closet you'll need protection from your own mother when she finds 'em.

When was the last time you considered the awesome diversity of all the plants, insects, mammals and reptiles around you? I believe the day to day display of planet Earth testifies to the power and omnipotence of our Heavenly Father. Yea, I know we're all busy, but come on, let's find a minute to inspect a ladybug, marvel at the whale and gaze at the clouds. And in doing so, let His creation turn our attention to the Creator for surely, "The whole earth is full of His glory!"

Shellie Rushing Tomlinson

The day to day display
of planet Earth testifies
to the power and omnipotence
of our Heavenly Father.

"It's a Relationship"

I used to know a lady who was always moving from one church to another. The truth is, the churches weren't the problem. She was just miserable. You see, she knew too much about the Lord to be happy outside of church—but her unwillingness to give in to God's will for her life caused her to be miserable inside church, any church. Poor lady, she was stretched so tight trying to hold onto her world with one hand and the church with the other that she was always prone to losing her grip—one of them, anyway.

Can you identify with the lady in my story? I can! For years I wanted Jesus to be my Savior, (for eternity), but I wasn't willing to let Him be my Lord, (here on earth). Can I be honest? Trying to live the Christian walk can be the most miserable experience in the world—if there is no Christ in your experience. It's true and I'm not trying to split hairs. I just want you to see that the power to live the Christian life comes from a relationship with Jesus, not a church building.

If you've never given up and given your whole heart to Him, what do you have to lose? Instead of trying to "be good", (which is way outside our capabilities), you can enjoy dwelling on how good He is. Instead of trying to live *for* Him you can enjoy living *with* Him, talking to Him every day just like you do everyone else around you.

How about it? "Oh, taste and see that the Lord is good. Blessed is the man that trusts in Him." Psalms 34:8

*The Christian experience
can be most miserable
if there is no Christ
in your experience.*

"Racing, Face Down?"

It was the morning of the big elementary track meet and I was
ready for my first race of the day—the 100-yard dash. My
classmate Lenny Ray, who now runs an Internet gambling site, had
me the heavy favorite. I had mile-long legs for goodness sakes and
I was, if I might say so, quite the sought after player for any game
of dodge ball or Red Rover.

The gun sounded! I was slow out of the blocks, but once I got
those legs started, I passed the whole group-heading to the finish
line neck and neck with one of the boys! Deep in my soul, I knew I
was going too fast! I felt the first inkling of a trip and struggled to
hold on, but alas, I went down amidst a sea of legs (all my own) in
total humiliation, five steps from victory.

Sometimes that happens to me in my spiritual walk too. Have you
ever been out front, racing towards Jesus with a head of steam,
only to find yourself somehow, surprisingly, lying face down in the
ground with a mouthful of dust? It happens—but here's the good
news. Unlike my loyal supporters who laughed themselves silly,
the One who called you in the first place is right there waiting. God
won't count you out, and if you look to Him for hope and
forgiveness, He'll strengthen you to get back up and try again. Who
knows, I might could've won the next race if I wouldn't have went
and hid under the bleachers...

The One who calls you
won't count you out.
He'll strengthen you
to try again.

"Facing Changes"

Things are different around the Tomlinson house these days. I've always liked to say that folks that can't accept change will eventually end up like the grouchy old people the movies like to stereotype. Isn't it fun when the Lord lets you test your theories? You see, I did pretty well when I had to realize that I couldn't have babies forever to keep that "infant in the house" feeling. So I poured myself into my kids' childhood. And I know it's unusual but we actually enjoyed their teenage years. Still, as well prepared for change as I thought I was, this latest one has knocked me a little off center. Now that Phillip has joined his sister Jessica at college, Phil and I are official empty nesters.

There are a lot of positives about this new phase of my life, so it's not that I'm sad really. It's just weird. At the close of the first few days, I couldn't shake the feeling that I'd forgotten to do something important, like I hadn't fulfilled all the day's responsibilities.

Maybe you're reeling from one of life's unexpected turn of events. Or maybe, like me, the change wasn't a surprise, but you're still trying to find your footing. I'll share my secret with you: lean ever closer to the One that never changes. Jesus Christ, the same, yesterday, today and tomorrow. Regardless of the twists and turns in your path, He wants to be your Solid Rock. Now, how good does that sound?

*Lean ever closer to
the One that never changes.*

"Troublesome Moral Faults"

One day I was sitting in my parked car outside a public building waiting to give a friend a ride. My daughter Jessica, who was about four at the time, was perched on the console beside me. We had all the windows down to allow a little air to stir. About that time, a lady who will remain nameless strolled towards my vehicle. Although I knew from past experience that she probably wouldn't speak, I smiled and gave her my usual friendly greeting. And like so many times before, she gave me what I call a "social smile." I reckon it means, "Hi. I'm fine, thanks, leave me alone," but the world will never know because her lips never part. That particular day it really got to me. Lowering my voice, I murmured "snot"—commenting on the lady's attitude you understand, not any sort of nasal discharge. Jessica whirled around but since all she could see was the lady's back so she asked me innocently, "Was it all over her face, mama, or just on her nose?"

I thought of this story recently when I was reading in Galatians. My amplified Bible says it this way, "Bear with one another's troublesome moral faults and so fulfill and observe the law of Christ." You do know why we should be forbearing don't you? Because we get the same type of judgment we give out. That's another of the Bible's principles and although I might not see my troublesome moral faults as clearly as I do the faults of others, they're there—and you can always trust your kids to show you the egg, or snot, on your own face.

Southern Comfort

*We will get back
the same type
of judgment
we give out.
Ouch!*

"Finding Yourself Isn't So Tricky"

When I was a young girl folks around the country began finding themselves. They weren't physically lost, that was just the popular term of the day—it was actually about finding the meaning to your life. Still, I remember how funny we thought it was when one young lady we knew left her parents home to go and find herself.

I guess "finding yourself" was just funny to our southern ears. For around here, we're BIG on knowing who we are. "Who are your people" and "where 'ya from" follow any introductions. Roots are important and the family tree is full of first, second and third cousins as well as those cousins who are once removed. Sorry, I can't get into the complications of "once removed." We don't have time.

While it's true my name is Shellie Rushing Tomlinson and I'm from Bull Run Road in Alsatia, Louisiana, that's only a small part of the story. Far more importantly, I'm from the heart of God. My life was planned and purposed from the foundation of the earth. And so was yours, my friend. You are God's creation, born out of His great love. Knowing that you're here on purpose and not by accident can be motivating and inspiring. If you're looking to find yourself start there, at the beginning—the rest will fall into place.

*Your life was planned
and purposed
from the foundation
of the earth.*

"Unexpressed Fears Can Be Hairy"

Sometimes little kids ask questions that don't accurately reveal what they're really thinking. If they ask you why Papaw has hair growing out of his ears, they don't actually mean why, they're probably just wondering if they're going to wake up the next morning with the same condition. I know this because I can remember how my mind worked as a child.

When I was a little girl growing up on Bull Run Road I worried about going to jail. I remember being afraid I'd accidentally break the law. Anytime a new law was identified for me—like littering for example, or shooting a deer out of season, my fears would resurface. And I'd pester Mama with endless questions: "How did grownups know what to do and what not to do?" "Where were all the rules written?" Had I ever articulated my actual fears to Mama, she could've saved me a lot of sleepless nights.

Oftentimes big people have unexpressed fears, too. Some folks hesitate to turn their lives over to the Lord because they're afraid of failing. They've heard a lot about the rules and they're not sure they're up to the whole Christian thing. Frankly, we haven't done such a great job of sharing His message. The Christ centered life is about a relationship between God and man. Don't hesitate at the Cross because you don't know the rules. Seek the Ruler Himself and you'll find that His word will be a lamp unto your feet and a light unto your path.

Southern Comfort

*The Christ centered life
is about a relationship
between you and your father.
Don't hesitate at the Cross
because you're unsure of the rules.*

~*~

172

"If I Were God..."

If I were God...I would protect the people that loved me from all the evil in the world. If I were God, I'd make sure that nothing bad every happened. I'd make sure that only good things happen to good people and then ALL the people would love me and serve me and obey me. And life would be heaven on earth. Oh, that's right, He did that already.

God gave his creation a Garden and filled it with everything good. And then he "allowed" man to disobey. Have you ever thought about that? The only reason man could disobey was because God refused to withhold anything from his creation, the dream of His heart that he fashioned out of dust. His greatest gift of love was to allow them the choice to know Him in an intimate relationship. Their free will was a gift; they were never compelled to love Him. Had God withheld their free will, his creation would've been puppets.

Our free will, yours and mine, is a precious gift of God. Every individual receives it at birth. We have to choose to serve God. But with this free will comes all the thorns and snares of life on earth. Can I share a little phrase with you that gets me through the tough spots? Maybe it'll bring you comfort. It's called "Father Filtered" and it means your Father has allowed whatever troubling circumstance you find yourself or your loved ones facing.

173

God is good and life is hard. Faith is accepting both truths and holding tightly to the first in the face of the second.

Shellie Rushing Tomlinson

*Faith accepts
that God is good
and life is hard.*

"Chicken Little, My Way"

This morning I noticed the heavily laden pecan trees in my backyard and it reminded me to tell y'all my own Chicken Little story. One day my mom took my sisters and me to a local pecan orchard to pick up pecans and make our own Christmas spending money.

We were instructed to stay on a certain line of trees. Of course, I thought the trees a few rows over had more pecans. I had wandered over there and was busy filling my sack when the sky started falling. Okay, it didn't really start falling. I just thought it had. Actually, a man on a tree-shaking machine had grabbed the trunk and commenced to giving it a good shake. My small presence had gone undetected.

Mama says that once she calmed me down, she was torn between wanting to hug me and spank me. I didn't care. I was just thankful for being in her arms. That big loud machine didn't look so much like a kid-eating monster from her lap.

Just like the story of Chicken Little—the sky wasn't falling on my head. I just needed some perspective. Once I was removed from the situation I could see what was causing all the trouble. So, I'm just saying: if it seems like your sky is falling, step back into your Heavenly Father's arms. It might not change your circumstances, but it'll give you a better handle on it. And sometimes, well, sometimes you can see how far you've wandered from the right line of trees.

~*~

*Stepping back into your
Father's arms doesn't
always change the situation,
but it will always give
you a better handle
on the circumstance.*

"Keeping Secrets"

There are times when half the fun of having a secret is making sure someone knows you're keeping one. I remember when my kids were small and Jessica and Philip would try to keep secrets from me at Christmas. Jessica would say things like, "I can't tell you what we got you for Christmas. It's a secret, huh, Sillip?" Her brother Phillip would nod his little blond head vigorously. All the while, their eyes would be begging me to plead with them for full disclosure.

I can see my Heavenly Father in that picture. Although you might be surprised to hear this, the Lord has a secret, too. And just like Jessica and Phillip, He longs to share it. Psalms 25:14 tells us that those that fear and worship the Lord know the secret of His sweet, satisfying companionship.

I like to think that the Lord mentions His secret just to whet our appetite, kind of like my little kids once did. He wants to have a fulfilling, life-giving relationship with all of His children. The problem lies on our end. For the Father also said, "You shall seek me and you shall find me when you seek for me with all your heart." That's not a casual search, folks. And that's why His sweet and satisfying companionship often remains a secret. Please, don't let it be true in your life. Trust me, this is one secret you're going to want to be in on.

Those that fear
and worship the Lord
know the secret of
His satisfying relationship.

"My Best Friend"

How's the world treating you? Need the shoulder of a good friend? I'll share my friend with you—He's the best!

In John 15:15 Jesus said, "Henceforth, I call you not servants, but friends. For all things I've heard of my Father I've made known to you."

I believe it's crucial to our relationships with Jesus for us to believe He wants to be our friend. If we don't believe He is sensitive to our problems, we won't turn to Him in prayer.

Most of us have acquaintances and friends. We don't call our acquaintances with our problems because although most of them would listen politely, we know they won't really get involved emotionally. But we do call our FRIENDS—people we know will immediately respond to the hurt in our voices and offer their heartfelt support! We ring these folks up without a second thought.

Our relationship with the Father works the same way. Only when we truly believe the words found in Psalms 145:18, "God is near to all that call upon him," will we bear our hearts to Him and realize His comforting presence.

*If we don't believe
He is sensitive
to our problems,
we won't turn
to Him in prayer.*

"Adjusted Attitudes"

I was minding my own business this morning, looking up some scriptures about giving thanks and being grateful, when suddenly I had a Bull Run Road flashback accompanied by the voice of my mama, "You better watch your attitude." You see, moping and sulking were forbidden at our house. My sisters and I learned to count our blessings right along with our fingers and toes. We could never throw a successful pity party around our parents. This was really irritating during our teenage years. Here's another of Mama's famous lines, "If you don't adjust your attitude, I'll do it for you." Listen, we might not have been the brightest kids on the block, but we had enough sense to figure out that it was always less painful to adjust our attitudes before Mama took a turn at 'em.

Which brings me back to where I was before my flashback… Did you realize that our Heavenly Father requires us to have grateful hearts, attitudes of gratitude, so to speak? All of those verses in His word about giving thanks—they're commands, not suggestions! I'm just reminding you, while I remind myself, that attitude adjustments are always easier on the front end. Now, let me leave you with the promise that comes with the command. Philippians 4:6 tells us that if you won't fret or worry, but in every circumstance make your request known to God with thanksgiving, His peace will guard your hearts and minds. Simply put, seeds of thanksgiving will reap a harvest of peace. Hmmm...Sounds like a good deal to me.

~*~

Seeds of thanksgiving
will reap a
harvest of peace...

~*~

"Shared Treasures"

I was at a friend's house the other day when her little girls came in with some "treasures" they'd found in the backyard. Their loot looked pretty average, a few well-formed pinecones and a handful of pretty leaves, but they had big plans. The big sister was going to help the little one take their goodies and make Christmas ornaments.

Do you remember searching for treasure? I do! I remember scouring the woods behind my grandparents' house looking for Indian arrowheads. Thanks to my older sister's storytelling ability I always kept one eye out just in case any of those viscous Injuns circled back! And once, after studying rock formations in school, I spent a whole afternoon digging through the pea gravel in our driveway, fully expecting to find a mysterious fossil.

I never had much luck searching for hidden treasure—at least not the material kind, but I've found something far more valuable. Isaiah 33: 6 says the fear and worship of the Lord is your treasure and His. This is one shared treasure I can vouch for. Oh, and those sweet little girls—well, I'm now the proud owner of one exquisite pine cone ornament. Soon, I'll place in a prominent place on my family tree, in honor of my young friends and to remind myself of the eternal treasure that's available to us all!

Southern Comfort

*Have you found
the eternal treasure
available to us all?*

"Losing Track of Time"

I woke up this morning with a turkey stuffed stomach and a one-track mind—focused on decorating for Christmas. The atmosphere was perfect. It was cold; Phil had a roaring fire going in the fireplace, and both of the kids were home from college and sleeping in. I was feeling like a Hallmark Christmas Card! Before long I looked more like a mixed up Mother Goose. Up to the attic, down from the attic, here a room, there a room—around and around she goes and where she stops nobody knows.

I let the family fend for themselves at lunch and ignored the phone completely. I'm afraid I even neglected my hostess duties out here on the porch. Sorry! Late this afternoon, I stopped to admire my efforts. May I say it looked like a winter wonderland and the North Pole rolled up into one warm and fuzzy display? There was only one problem. It suddenly occurred to me that I was freezing!

And that, friends, is the first time I noticed the fire had gone out in the fireplace. As far as I know, it could've been out for ages! So, here's the lesson. (You knew I'd see a lesson, didn't you?) This same thing can happen in our spirits. It's easy to get so busy with the holiday's activities and responsibilities that we let the real meaning of Christmas die down and burn out in our hearts, until one day we wake up cold and dry! So, come on. Let's all remember to open the Scriptures regularly and throw a log on our fires. Time spent with the Father will keep our homes and our hearts warm and toasty.

187

~*~

Opening the scriptures regularly
will throw a log on your fire
and keep your heart warm.

"Take your Medicine, Folks"

Several nights ago we got together with some friends to play a board game. It was me and Phil with our kids Jessica and Phillip, Phillips girlfriend Carey and our friends Rhonda and Lamar with their kids, Jake and Jami-Lynn. The game was *Cranium*. Rhonda and I wanted to team up, partly because we knew wed win, but mostly to avoid partnering with Phil and Lamar. We weren't being ugly; we just have a lot experience playing games like that with our husbands.

Phil and Lamar will give you one clue. If you don't get it, their idea of helping you is to circle it again and again. We laughed at them all night. Oh, and my kids made fun of me because they said I sermonized while giving Phil the clues for Madonna. I don't know what they're talking about, all I said in my description was, I like material things and I don't have any morals.

And then there was the triple J team, Jessica, Jake and Jami-Lyn. They made the rest of us sick. One of them would make the first line of a leg and the others would shout shin splints—and they'd be right! It was disgusting and very, very funny.

I bring this up because I'm reminded of the scripture in Proverbs that says laughter doeth good like a medicine. It's such a beautiful truth and one of Gods great gifts to us. Don't neglect the power of laughter. If nothing else, play a word game with your husband. It works every time.

Shellie Rushing Tomlinson

*Laughter—it's good medicine
and one of God's great gifts
to His children. Don't forget
to take a daily dose...*

"Recharge Your Batteries"

This sweet new puppy of mine is seven weeks old now and already Dixie Belle and I are incredibly bonded! We've actually fallen into some sort of routine in the last week, too. I sit at my computer and try to keep an eye on her while she terrorizes her chew toys and plays herself down to a frazzle. Then she comes looking for me. Dixie likes nothing more than resting at my feet, unless it's on feet. Of course, after these little downtimes she is more the hyper-kinetic, chewing puppy than ever before—but hey—that's what she was designed to be.

I thought about Dixie's habits earlier when I was doing a bit of Bible reading. With all of my responsibilities, it's not always easy to fit that in, but I'm determined to because I've found a secret. Those times with the Father, just resting in his presence, reenergize me and allow me to tackle my to-do list.

Did you know there's a scripture in Isaiah that says, "In returning and rest shall you be saved, in quietness and in confidence shall be your strength but you would not." That's a tragedy that could be easily avoided. Do yourself a big favor. Find some time; make some time to get to know the Lord. Rest at his feet and hear him say in the Psalm, "Be still and know that I am God." You'll not only recharge your batteries, but afterwards, you can be everything you were meant to be.

Shellie Rushing Tomlinson

Here's a secret:
Rest in His presence
and you'll find
the energy you need
to tackle your to-do list...

"Let Him Grow Up"

When I was a little girl, Christmas took forever to make its way to Bull Run Road. Not anymore, it seems like it was just yesterday when I pulled the boxes down from the attic and began pulling out the nativity scene, the miniature lights and the keepsake ornaments. And now, just that fast—it's Christmas. Soon the tree will be naked, the presents long gone. It'll be hard to remember who got what from whom and I'll start packing all the decorations away for another year.

I was sitting here thinking about how bare and cold the house will look when I realized that sadly, this scene would play itself out in many hearts as well. Many people will have had expectations that weren't filled and many of those will be left with hurts that won't heal. Unless this year is different, it's my bet that the newspapers will soon be talking about depression and the talk shows will have experts on to offer ways to fill the long days ahead and cure the winter blues.

I'm no expert, but I'd like to offer a suggestion that will go beyond the creature comforts of a warm bath or a bowl of hot soup. Your heart doesn't have to be bare and naked after the holidays. Do you want to know the real secret? Don't pack up the Christ Child with Christmas. As beautiful and special as the Christmas story is, it's only a part of heaven's miracle. The Christ child grew into a man; the man became the Savior.

194

Shellie Rushing Tomlinson

This year, let the baby from Bethlehem grow up in your hearts. Allow him to become the Messiah He was born to be and the joy of Christmas will be yours all year long.

~*~

The Christ child
became a man;
the man
became the Savior...

~*~

"Dream Big"

Think back to your childhood days. Remember when grownups asked you that timeless question, "What you want to be when you grow up?" The possibilities seemed endless, didn't they? No decision had been made, no college majors chosen, the world was yours.

A lot has happened since then, hasn't it? Life has happened. Somewhere along the line you decided that all your choices have been chosen and your path determined. It's not true. What makes you think that where you are today is where you have to stay? Your Heavenly Father hasn't drawn those boundaries. He created your spirit to soar.

Have you buried a dream? Have you lost that sense of hope? If so, I'd like to encourage you to turn to Jesus, the giver of Hope. Your Heavenly Father says, "I know the plans I have for you, to give you a future and a hope." Those plans don't come with an expiration date. The Lord your God made you special and unique, different from every other person in the world. There is no other you and no one that can accomplish your special mission on this earth. Seek Him. Don't settle with New Year's resolutions that will simply change your appearance. Reach for the very heart of God and let him change your life from the inside out.

New Year's is a wonderful time to dream, so dream big! Get alone with your Heavenly Father and let Him lead you step by step into your future. Let him remind you of the dream. I ask you, regardless of your chronological age, "What do you want to be when you grow up?"

Shellie Rushing Tomlinson

Don't settle for resolutions
that only change your appearance;
reach for the heart of God
and let Him change you
from the inside out!

"Where is Your Rope Tied?"

Between dire news about the economy and warnings of terrorist threats, the evening news can be disconcerting at best.

I'm reminded of a poster we've all seen. Remember the cat hanging onto the end of a rope? The caption read something like, "When you get to the end of your rope, tie a knot and hang on!"

That's good advice, but I want to take it a step further. In the poster you can't see what the rope is tied to. It could be a strong and sturdy tree with a deep root system—but then it could be a little twig. Uh-oh kitty!

Maybe you're holding on tight. Great! But where is your rope tied?

I think our current president is doing an excellent job—but I'm not tying my rope to the White House. And I think our soldiers are the best of the rest—but I'm not tying my rope to their skill and courage. No way! My rope is tied behind the veil. Hebrews 6:19 talks about the hope we have as an "anchor of our souls, both sure and steadfast entering into that within the veil, where the forerunner is for us entered, even Jesus..." Wow, right behind Jesus? Now, there's a good place to tie a lifeline!

The message of hope is also found in Psalms 42:11. "Why art thou cast down, O my soul? And why are though disquieted within me?

Hope thou in God, for I shall yet praise Him, who is the salvation and my God."

Southern Comfort

~*~

*Where is your
rope tied?*

~*~

202

"The Christian Adventure"

The other evening I took a walk with my friend, Rhonda. At one point, when I was busy talking, Rhonda broke in and pulled me and my right foot back just before I stepped on a ground rattler. Together, we grabbed some nearby bricks and killed it.

Our Christian lives are a lot like this snake adventure. There're many reasons why the Lord said not to forsake the assembling of yourselves together. For instance, sometimes if you're distracted, a friend in Christ can help you see the danger you're headed towards and "pull" you back through prayer and wise counsel. Even after a passing car ran over our dead snake, his nerves still allowed him to coil into a striking pose. Guess who else is defeated, but roars around like he's not? Would you like a hint? He took the form of a snake once, too. Right! You know, our Savior defeated Satan for us, but we can't take part in His victory without kneeling at His Cross.

Once you've knelt at the Cross, don't neglect Christian fellowship. You won't regret it and you might find it comes in handy.

*We can't take part
in the Savior's victory
without kneeling
at the Cross...*

~*~

"Running into Walls"

Once I was sitting at my computer working when I heard a loud noise. Whoomp! Jessica and I got up and walked over to the big bay window beside my desk. (I recently moved my desk to the living room so I could have more time with my family.)

We found a very stunned little bird, a tufted titmouse, sitting on the pavement below the window. I felt like I knew him, because my bird feeder is right outside the window and I'd been watching a whole family of titmice for the past few weeks. My little friend sat there so long that I walked outside to see if he was dead. He was motionless as I knelt down and picked him up. His eyes were barely moving and it looked like one of his feet might be broken. For a moment he allowed me to hold him, but when I stood up he flew right back toward the window pane that had just knocked him senseless and fluttered there, trying to get through the glass. I picked him back up a little more forcefully this time, and took him back in the right direction, to more familiar territory, the birdfeeder. Mr. Titmouse sat there for a few minutes, regaining his senses before he grabbed a snack and flew off.

And so I wondered. (You knew I would.) I think I know just how Mr. Titmouse felt. I've ran headlong into things that I never saw coming before—and I've even ignored the One that could help me and banged my head right back into the thing that knocked me down in the first place.

Southern Comfort

How about you? Have you hit any walls or windows lately? Are you still banging your head against the glass? God is ready and willing to point you back in the right direction. But you will have to settle down and trust Him.

Shellie Rushing Tomlinson

How about it?
Are you banging your
head against the glass,
because you refuse
to let Him point you
in the right direction?

"What's Growing in Your Fields?"

Let's play a game of pretend. Tomorrow morning you get up and eat four Krispy Kreme doughnuts for breakfast. Wham! Wham! Wham! Wham! With each doughnut you can see a new roll added to the spare tire around your middle. Whoa! You decide you had better start a new exercise program, so you warm up, stretch, and proceed to walk two miles pumping hand weights. Before you can even get back home your shorts are a size too big, your leg muscles are toned and your biceps are well defined. Hey, this is great! Let's take it up a notch.

Later that morning you run into Jane at the water cooler. She mentions that Betty has on a new outfit and she looks great. since you never really liked Betty, you casually mention that you heard Betty's register has come up short quite a few times lately. Suddenly, Betty comes running by both of you crying. It seems a rumor made its way back to the boss that Betty was stealing from the company. Now, she's out of a job! Oh, no—surely not from your remark—you barely got the words out of your mouth.

Although most of us know the principle of sowing and reaping, the growing season between the two often lulls us into forgetting that our actions have consequences. We find it easier to believe we've run into a streak of bad luck, or our metabolism is slow, or the enemy is attacking us...than face the facts that we're reaping a harvest of long forgotten seeds.

Shellie Rushing Tomlinson

The Bible says we're always sowing, either to the spirit or to the flesh. Wouldn't it be great to have a warning on our bag of seeds? Something like: "Caution! These are painful words, once full grown they'll reap a broken relationship!" Well, do I have good news for you! We do have such a guide—it's called the Bible. Think of it as God's version of the Farmer's Almanac, overflowing with advice on what you should and shouldn't plant. Come on, let's get knee deep in the Word. I don't know about you, but I'm determined to learn to control my impulses before I plant seeds I have no desire to harvest.

*The Bible, God's version
of the Farmer's Almanac.
Let it help you plant the right seeds
at the right time.*

~*~

"Dixie Belle and Juicy Fruit"

Had you seen us, you probably would've laughed, but it wasn't
funny at the time. I'd been working hard at my desk for an hour or
so without interruption from Dixie Belle, who I knew to be at my
feet on her pillow. Good puppy...or so I thought until I stopped for
a cup of coffee and found the evidence of her mischief. Someone,
that would be me, had unwisely disposed of some chewing gum in
the trash can. Dixie Belle had found it. Now it was strung out all
over her face, her whiskers, her coat, and all four little bear-like
foot pads. Thus decorated, Dixie was now stretched out fast asleep,
obviously exhausted from trying to extricate herself from the mess.
I'm not really surprised that she managed to stay so quiet during
her trial. The thing is: she'd already been scolded for being in the
trash can. Without giving her too much credit here, I really think
she knew she was in even more trouble and had tried to get herself
out before I found her. I remember removing gum from my
children's hair with peanut butter. Comparatively speaking, that
was a breeze. At least *they* weren't trying to eat it as I worked.

While I scrubbed on Dixie I thought of how we much smarter
humans often make such a mess out of our lives—and then
complicate the problem by hiding from the Lord, so to speak, and
trying to clean our own selves up. It doesn't work for us any better
than it did for Dixie and it's ever bit as exhausting, spiritually and
physically. The Bible teaches that if we confess our sins and look
to Christ for forgiveness, we can be washed clean but if we deny

211

our sins, we'll die in them. And that, my friends, is a fate far worse than the sticky mess Dixie found herself in today. If you need a good, long bath, don't hide—run...straight to the Father.

Shellie Rushing Tomlinson

Trying to clean our own
self up is fruitless.
It's also exhausting,
spiritually and physically.
To be eternally clean—
run to the Father...

"In Grandma's Eyes"

Last week I stumbled across an old photo of me sitting at a little typewriter and the memories came flooding back. I must have been about ten or eleven. The typewriter was a Christmas gift from my grandmother on Papas side.

Grandma Rushing lived to be ninety-two and she enjoyed a full life, raising ten kids of her own and one that wasn't hers but should've been. She didn't have much formal education to speak of, but she was sharp, sharp as a tack we said. And she was proud of my infatuation with words. She loved to see me read books. I must have made her plenty happy because I read 'em by the truckload.

Grandma surprised me with the typewriter, telling me to write down my own words. She believed in me. She just knew I'd grow up to be a famous writer. Grandma Rushing is gone now, and I'm not a famous writer. I wasn't even doing All Things Southern when she left us. But that's okay; her gift to me was her belief in me. I'll always remember how tall I felt in Grandmas eyes.

Every child needs that. No, let's improve on that idea. Everyone, regardless of their age, needs someone who gives them that type of support. You can be that someone for the people in your life. Its scriptural you know. The Bible teaches us to be encouragers, to spur on and stimulate each other to good works. Oh—and guess what else? The Bible also teaches that what you measure out to others, you'll receive back with more added to it. Wow! You'll have to excuse me, I've got to find someone to encourage!

*Everyone needs someone
who believes in them.
You can be that someone
for the people in your life.*

"Talent and the Lack Thereof"

Some of the folks auditioning for these TV talent shows are so bad you have to wonder if it's a setup, like maybe they're only there to provide good targets for the quips and criticisms of the judges. If these contestants were serious about their singing aspirations, someone in their family would've stopped em before they got on national TV. At least that's the way it worked in my world.

On the other hand, I definitely understand their desire to perform. Maybe you've heard me mention my lifetime desire to sing like Loretta Lynn. I don't need to sing for Simon to see that's not going to happen. As a kid, I bemoaned the fact that I couldn't sing and everyone else in my musically gifted family could. Why? I'd ask my southern Mama, who would soothe my hurt feelings by pointing out that I had good hair. Good hair or not, I wanted to sing and I complained to anyone who would listen that the whole thing was grossly unfair!

As a mature adult, I no longer think that some things in life are unfair. I know they are! But that's okay, because I know that where it really matters, we all start out shoulder to shoulder. The word says that each man is given a measure of faith to believe in God. Look at that a minute. You've been given the same measure of faith that Billy Graham was born with, or Mother Teresa. In other words, unlike a game show with an intimidating judge, the only hindrance in your developing an intimate relationship with the Father is the one you yourself allow. You can be a winner in the only game that matters: Life!

Shellie Rushing Tomlinson

In your capacity to believe,
you stand shoulder to shoulder
with Billy Graham and Mother Teresa.
What are you doing with your gift?

"Planning for the Future"

One of my porchers sent me the following story a while back. It seems an exasperated mother, whose son was always getting into mischief, finally asked him, "Johnny, how do you expect to get into heaven?"

The boy thought it over and said, "Well, I'll just run in and out and in and out and keep slamming the door until St. Peter says, 'For heaven's sake, Johnny! Come in or stay out!'"

If eternity wasn't a reality, I could enjoy this little story a whole lot more. Unfortunately, all you have to do is watch the news to see that plenty of people have even stranger notions on how to get there from here. And just as tragic, there are others who are so occupied with the cares of this life that they've yet to do even the limited planning of our young friend Johnny.

I know I'm not going to sound very politically correct here, but can I tell you what's on my heart? Regardless of whether you're the nicest, most moral person on this planet or mean as a striped snake, I understand God's word to say that there is still only one way to heaven—through belief in his son, Jesus. But, please, I'm not asking you to take my word for it. I'm praying you'll seek God for yourself, read His word, ask Him for the Truth, and make your travel plans accordingly.

Shellie Rushing Tomlinson

*There is still only
one way to heaven—
belief in Jesus,
God's only son.
Have you made your
travel plans?*

If you've enjoyed *Southern Comfort*, you might enjoy Shellie's memoir, *Lessons Learned on Bull Run Road*. You can purchase it online at http://www.allthingssouthern.com. Here's a FREE sample chapter.

LESSON NUMBER ONE
"Play Now or Pay Later"

Mama taught us to appreciate people's differences...

Poor Mama, she exhausted herself trying to smooth the rough edges of her little girls. Mama was a true "Southern lady", a natural beauty born the second of five to a Baptist preacher in Natchez, Mississippi. Her innate grace helped make her a basketball star; her black hair and bright wide smile topped a tall slender frame and earned her the hometown title of "Miss Forestry Queen."

Mama's marriage to her high school sweetheart ended shortly after she brought me, her third daughter, home from the hospital. Biological Dad was more interested in cards and liquor than diapers and bottles. Mama was raising three little girls on a clerk's salary, when a young man she'd known as a child came to town and dropped by to pay her family a visit. It'd been years since he and Mama had seen one another. By this time Future Papa was fresh out of the service and farming a plot of land in Alsatia,

Louisiana. For the next year or more he made the two-hour trip to court Mama. My sisters and I were their ever-present chaperones. I was two, Rhonda was three and Cyndie was five. We rode in the back seat of Future Papa's car and sang along with Mama to Conway Twitty's new hit song, "Mississippi Woman, Louisiana Man."

It wasn't long before Papa married us, taking his prize bride and her tiny wedding party to the Delta to live on Bull Run Road. He built her a little white brick home with 900 square feet. She kept his castle spotless and worked beside him in the fields.

Mama looked as much a lady driving Papa's bean truck and grain cart during the day, as she did on the piano bench at Melbourne Baptist Church—twice on Sunday and once on Wednesday night. Manners were important to Mama; a theme most of her lectures centered on, as she constantly schooled us in the things little ladies did and did not do. Unfortunately for Mama, my sisters and I had a hard time differentiating between the two.

Mama should've had at least one little girl who was proper--someone who liked to dress up and play tea party. Instead, she got Cyndie, Rhonda, and Shellie, (that's me there on the end), three tomboys. Rhonda might've came the closest, everyone did call her Pretty Woman, but being the middle child and painfully shy, she didn't stand a chance—Cyndie and I took her down with us. Most of our capers were birthed in Cyndie's fertile mind, with me badgering Rhonda into being our unwilling accomplice.

When Mama wasn't cleaning house, cooking a big meal, or helping Papa in the field, she liked to have a lady friend over for coffee. Life on Bull Run Road was pretty isolated with only one other house for miles, and our cousin Jimmy Ray lived there. But, we'll get back to Jimmy later.

Our job was to play with the visiting lady's children. Most of the time we only had each other to play with, so Mama thought it should be a real treat to have new friends. My sisters and I thought our club was complete; and for the most part we considered these intruders weenies, babies, girly-girls.

One summer day an old friend of Mama's came to visit. Cyndie, and Rhonda and I eyed her daughter warily as she emerged from the car. Our assessment paused at her feet. One of our major criteria was the absence or presence of shoes. Unless it was the dead of winter we went barefoot, and we were suspicious of those that didn't. Our circle had a hierarchy, and those with the toughest soles were accorded the most respect. We smiled sweetly until the grownups went indoors and then we hit Visiting Girly-Girl with a little Bull Run Road initiation.

If she'd walk the side rails of the bridge by our house, we'd consider playing with her—an honorable test in our estimation. This bridge was probably ten to fifteen feet high, and walking its

rails never gave us a moment's pause. Many of our days were spent
there. In the spring, if the drainage ditch below was full of water,
the rail might be our tight rope and we the daring circus
performers. During the summer months, when the bed was dry and
cracked and strewn with the fragile, pinkish-white skeletons of
crawdads that had escaped my sisters and me in the spring, it
turned into our fort. We slid beneath the rails, and perched on the
sloping sides of the ditch, hiding from the marauding Indians.
Cyndie could describe those vicious red natives with their sharp
knives and penchant for blond hair in such detail that Rhonda, the
only fair head in our fort, would cry to go home and I'd end up
with nightmares.

Stoically, my sisters and I led our potential playmate to the site of
her evaluation. Upon our arrival Cyndie instructed me to assume
my position on the bridge's rail and demonstrate the initiation
requirement. Poor Mama! Just as we expected, our guest refused
and went tattling to her mother, like the baby we knew she was.
Visitor Lady, and her crying girly-girl on one side of the table, and
we three lined up like wooden soldiers on the other. We felt totally
justified, but you couldn't miss the message in Mama's eyes: "Play
now or pay later."

Mama excused herself and took us to the back room. She explained
that there were many different kinds of people in the world and we
better find a way to get along with the ones that weren't just like
us. She said there was something you could learn from everyone

you met and something about most of them that you could enjoy, if
you gave him or her the chance. Then she glanced towards Papa's
belt on the dresser and smiled encouragingly. We decided then and
there to give Visiting Girly-Girl another chance.

*All the ways of a man are clean in his own eyes, but the Lord
weighs the motives.* Proverbs 16:2

Shellie's working on a new book and you can be a part of it.

WHAT SOUTHERN MOMS TELL THEIR DAUGHTERS…A
friend's mother gave her this piece of advice on her wedding night:
Honey, when you're late with supper, or just plain tired, remember
to have the Holy Trinity of Southern cooking (onions, celery and
bell pepper) sautéing in a dab of butter or bacon grease when your
man comes home—it'll put him in a good mood and you can feed
him anything. Shellie Rushing Tomlinson (author of *Lessons
Learned on Bull Run Road*) wants your southern mom's advice
about love, marriage, relationships and life in general. Write to
Shellie at tomtom@allthingssouthern.comto have your mom's
advice memorialized in her new book, WHAT SOUTHERN
MOMS TELL THEIR DAUGHTERS…

CPSIA information can be obtained
at www.ICGtesting.com
Printed in the USA
BVOW03s0628221117
500944BV00001BA/28/P